Abandonment Wounds

Understanding Self-Abandonment and Self-Sabotage

Jayne Payne, Ph.D.

Author's Note

Jayne wishes to make clear that this book is purely written as her own journey of reconnecting and in no way is it a scientific research book and a reflection of her various licenses.

Contents

Acknowledgments

This book is dedicated in loving memory of Dr. Ned Johnson, my companion for over twenty years. In loving memory of my parents who did the best they could and knew how out of love.

To my son Mark who is and always will be my hero, and the person I most admire. To his partner Michael who has shown me what true compassion is all about.

To my stepson Steven who has taught me that love can come at the most unexpected times in our lives.

To Ronald L. Digins for his creative art work and his gentle push to step up to the plate and pushing me to complete my book by letting me regain insight to the fact that if we all wait till things are perfect they never get done.

For my loving friend Nereida for her unwavering support and belief in the process of life, helping me edit, and get it together. For the loving support of Zulma and Ricardo and their commitment to help in the process. For Sophia, Steve, and her family who have taught me that it's possible for anyone to heal and learn to love again and reunite through the courage and perseverance of working through their abandonment wounds. To witness this has given me the incentive to complete this book. My undying gratitude to Iliana, David, and her entire family for their encouragement throughout the process and for the many others, who know who they are, and know how much they are loved and respected.

Last but surely not least, to all of you who are still searching for your inner peace, suffering from the pain of abandonment wounds and self-sabotage, a disconnect of your spiritual self, and not knowing why. I hope that somewhere in this book your light bulb will go on, restoring you to your connection with God, for it is there that you will find your true peace and purpose in life....the destiny you were sent to fulfill.

It is with great with a great deal of love and respect that I wish to pay a special tribute to Nerada Gomez. Without her believing in my Abandonment theory and Intensive Healing the Wounds program this book would probably never have been published. Her dedication and support over the years has been the paramount reason I continue to be aware that others can benefit from the Intensive Healing the Wounds weekend. I thank her for her contribution of the final chapter, testimonial, and organization of my cumulative information and development of the Abandonment Theory that is helping in the success of individuals struggling to find their inner peace and move forward with their lives. There are not enough words to express my gratitude.

—Jayne Payne

For all those who still suffer from the endless cycle of grief and pain perpetuated by unresolved issues of abandonment wounds. May you find your missing 'peace' at last.

My contribution to this book is dedicated in loving memory of my uncle Juan Bucio who loved dearly and whose mission in my extended family's lives helped me press on through the darker to lighter days.

To my family whom I love very much. To my husband Horacio who has been my greatest teacher and companion of a lifetime. I am blessed to share the journey with him. To our sons, Rafael and Adrian. Each day they show me how to love and laugh. They have my heart. May these pages give them the depth of awareness a decade earlier than it came to me!

To my parents, Roberto and Maria L. Bucio, who have taught me that there is always a better day. Their marriage and their openness to learn and love in new ways have been a gift in my life. To my sister, Zulma, who has been my best friend for so long. We have shared so much together and this makes it a one-in-a-lifetime sisterhood. She has nudged me in small and big ways to share this work. She is forever my inspiration.

To Evelyn, Lupita, and Ruvi, who I admire greatly. God not only gave me a sister but three soul sisters that have shared and let me share our vulnerable, courageous moments. We speak the same language.

To Jayne, the teacher I will forever cherish and friend who held my hand when I needed one the most. Thank you.

—Nereida Bucio Gómez

Nereida Bucio Gómez is currently a literacy coach in an elementary school in Houston Independent School District. She has worked as a bilingual teacher and other teacher support positions for eighteen years.

As an educational consultant, she provides staff development in school districts in Houston and the surrounding area in reading and writing best practices.

She has also self-published reading and writing educational resources. She is married and has two sons

Buyer Beware

People that purchase personal improvement books are looking for some word, some sentence, or paragraph in the book to have such a profound effect on their lives that it will, in and of itself, change their lives forever. So as you pick up this book to purchase, a word of caution. You might be asking yourself as you thumb through the pages, looking for the word or phrase to jump out at you, "What will this book do for me that others I have bought in the past have not?" (How do I know that is what you intend to do? I know because that is exactly what I have done over and over for years). I will tell you right up front before you read any further. This book alone will do absolutely nothing for you.

I hope that this will save you a lot of time, energy, and pain. I spent a majority of my life searching in every direction known to man, to find and grasp the epiphany I was sure was always just right around the corner. It was definitely out there, if I only looked for it. Little did I know that even if it was staring me in the face, I would not have recognized it if it bit me. I just somehow knew it was there, and if I looked longer and harder, I would find it. It even crossed my mind as the epiphany eluded me more and more, that maybe this was just the meaning of life and when one found it, life would miraculously end. Finally, one's world would be complete. There were periods of time I would just say to heck with it. I'm tired of looking. I will just do nothing and wait for the end. There were even periods that I thought I might be able to speed up the process, but then I would wonder if the end wouldn't come if one speeded up the process.

What I can share with you are the lessons I did learn throughout this journey. One of the most important lessons I did learn is that nothing is free. There is always a cost. It requires some action by the one that is searching. However, if you feel the need to keep searching, be my guest. Let this book serve as one of your guides along the way. The action that is required to reach your inner peace can often be painful and rewarding at the same time. It is kind of like laughing and crying, not knowing where the end will be. But at least you finally know there is an end and a light at the end of the tunnel-one that you have managed to dig for yourself and is getting closer. With your hand on the switch, only you can control the speed and location of your destination.

So, buyer beware. If you truly want to stop your self-abandonment and heal your abandonment wounds to reach your inner peace, IT WILL REQUIRE ACTION FROM YOU! The paradox here is that the book will do nothing for you, but it will provide a road map for you to gain understanding of the reasons you have chosen the roads that you have traveled. With understanding comes knowing and with knowing comes new actions, with new actions comes new directions, with new direction comes new roads, with new roads comes a new, freeing life, and with a new and freeing life comes your inner peace. So until you are ready to take action and open the map, nothing will change. Reading this book will simply be a new and hopefully enlightening adventure, until you are ready to do what you need to do to make the changes you want to make. It is OK to be in the let me think about it stage. I sat there for many years, and that alone taught me a lot. Congratulations for making it this far.

Beware and get ready for change, for as the wise men say:

the truth will set you free.

The Inspiration and Motivation for change

In the twelve-step program, the saying is "You are only as sick as your secrets." My ego guarded them well for many years, with the false thought that it was protecting me, not hurting me. That I can tell you proved false. It was and continues to be the secrets that kept me self-sabotaging my life. There are life-changing events that also happen in everyone's life, and what we do with them will determine our future. We must all go within, and make a decision to follow our inner voice.

Having grown up in a not so functional family system, I learned at an early age I could not trust my own inner voice. I learned that I must always seek help from those that knew more than me such as my parents, older siblings, teachers, friends, etc. They were telling me my inner voice was wrong. That also started me in the search for the missing piece by seeking the truth from others and then being betrayed, which lead to not trusting others or myself — let alone God. I learned to never ever trust myself or ask God for guidance. I assumed my parents were God, and would only speak to me as God would. So everything they said to me, I believed was true. Because I was a child, it never occurred to me to filter the humanness of my parents from God's truth. Because my parents were God in providing me my survival, my shelter, my clothing, my food, my morals, my values, and my beliefs. In my mind, after all, He spoke through my parents, not me. Those were the messages a lot of us received growing up.

It has taken me most of my life to break the negative tapes and learn that I am the only one that can give me the true answers that are best for me, even though the results are not always what I would like. I lived with the illusion that I was in control. Learning that was an illusion, and being able to let go, was one of the most difficult lessons I have ever had to learn; because to let go meant letting go of my ego and all my self-worth was linked to that.

This book is part of letting go for me and giving up the illusion of control, ego, and all the negative past tapes that played in my head from those around me that told me You could never do it. You will never do it. You aren't smart enough. You don't have anything to offer. No one will be interested in what you have to say, and What do you know? Oh, and by the way, Nobody likes you.

This is a step out in faith and trust that something inside of me is greater than myself, and knows what I am here for and what my destiny is. I hope that you will be able to relate, learn, understand, and find your own inner voice that will help guide you out of the dark and into your light. We all have our own lights and my hope is this book will help you find and turn on your light. This book has come into being through the encouragement of the true friends I have in my life and the guidance of God. If the word God does not resonate with you, I'm sorry because it is only with God's help that my life has been changed and this book is now in your hands. What counts is where you end up.

Even though it is widely recognized as a serious problem for countless people around the world, up until now the core issue of abandonment has only been touched upon by psychologists, educators, and writers. It has never been fully explored and examined, let alone thoroughly analyzed and explained. As a human being, author, teacher, and a licensed therapist, my inspiration was derived from long years of working through my own life issues and with people from all walks of life who suffer from a vicious cycle of grief and pain that has been passed on from generation to generation.

In the process of sitting down to write this book it suddenly occurred to me that I could get to the problem and the solution in two short pages:

First page – Thank you to everyone that helped contribute to the content and for personal support in the writing of the book. Second page – The problem and the solution.

So now I not only have my answer about where to begin, I also have the ability to continue learning and growing from this exciting new adventure—one that I have actually been on all my life and hope will continue till the end. In seeking outside guidance, I did the very thing that helps a person turn within and begin to identify that they have become subconsciously engaged in self-abandonment. For only by reaching out and turning within can one stop abandoning one's self. Thus, it is both the problem and the solution.

In my book I will examine how the core issue of abandonment wounds affects people at every stage of their lives.

THE PROBLEM: Abandonment wounds = Self-Abandonment

How the core issue of abandonment affects people at every stage of their lives

THE SOLUTION: Turning within, you never go without. You connect with God and heal; you break the cycle of grief and pain.

Once in everyone's life we at some point have something to say. We hope that others can hear and learn from the experiences we have gone through. Some will hear and learn, others will hear and ignore. Both are OK. We are all on our own journey, and it is the journey and the lessons along the way that take us to our destiny. What counts is where we end up.

My partner once said, "It is not the material things in life that count. It is the relationship we have with others that counts most. In the end, we are all connected in the soul." He was so right! Having someone hearing our truths is a chance we all have to take if we are truly willing to.

Welcome to a new world! Narration of a First Encounter

UNDERSTANDING
SELF-ABANDONMENT

The cycle is breakable.

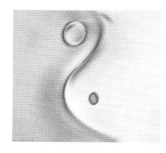

Right there in the delivery room we begin to learn, adopt, and initiate self-abandonment wounds; this in turn can cause a lifelong cycle of grief and pain.

Chapter 1

Out of the Delivery Room and Straight Into the Theatre of Life

IN THE BEGINNING...

came our core issues and beliefs that determine how we think and feel about our lives

and what we create in them

Everything we create comes from the beginning, and only by going back, and challenging our core beliefs can we change our feelings and responses to the world around us today. You see, a strange thing happened on the way to being born. Our first crisis occurred. Crisis is nothing more than a change that creates a feeling or belief that will make us move forward or backward in our lives. Our first crisis, or change, occurs at birth as we are being pushed, kicking, and screaming, out of our mother's womb.

The first response to a change that is occurring in our lives (whether we want it to or not) is the first time we experience fear of the unknown (thus we now link fear with change). I am being kicked out! What will happen to me? Will I survive? What will it be like out there? Oops, I'm slipping! Will someone catch me, or will I fall? (Our second fear). See how fear of life keeps building? This is the ultimate abandonment by our protector for the last nine months (if you were lucky enough to have nine months); and oh yes, the end all be all, no more free lunches. Like it or not, change from now on is going to be an ongoing thing.

So here you are a helpless newborn baby faced with the crisis of change taking place, and the first thing that greets you is a gigantic doctor in an immaculate white coat. (Some infants are so traumatized that they develop the White Coat Syndrome, fear causing all kinds of physical reactions even into adulthood when they see a doctor in a white coat). Then he or she slaps you on the butt (ow, that hurts), makes you cry, and sticks a tube in your mouth that feels like it's going to suck out your lungs. Frantically you think, "Is this person trying to kill me?" Next, the doctor turns to your mom and dad and says, "Congratulations, you have a boy!" or "Congratulations, you have a girl!" Of course, you are not privy to their response as you're now being moved about a brightly lit room, and they all seem to be totally unaware that you have never seen light before. What's more, they don't seem to care.

That's when a new thought occurs: oops, don't trust anyone. So whom can you trust? No one, and this creates even more fear. You don't get to see or hear if your parents are happy about you being a boy or a girl unless they were told beforehand from one of those privacy-invading ultrasound machines used to check to see if you're OK. You might have an inkling about whether or not your parents are happy, but somehow you have a hard time understanding their confusing messages. That's because you're not a rocket scientist yet, but they surely have hopes, or they would not have checked on you

Still more fear, "What if I am not OK? What will happen then?" So fear of abandonment, or if you like, the fear of doom, can even begin before birth. What pressure you're under already! But wait, you must be OK or else (it's the or else that really begins to scare you) the medical staff wouldn't be acting so confident and calm. It seems to be OK to be seen in your ugliest phases of life by a doctor pre-birth and birth. However, by the time you're being potty trained, you can't be seen or go out with dirty underwear. Life is so confusing, or is it just the messages people give us that are confusing?

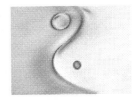

It is not change we fear but the consequences of change that make us fearful.

All of this creates our first response to change, which is fear. With this thought in mind it occurs to me that it is not change we fear, it is the consequences of change that makes us fearful. What will happen if . . .

Having just been abandoned, they then lay you on your mother's belly "to help you bond." Really, they are attempting to give you a short time to grieve over the safe and supportive place you were just pushed out of. The key is, short grief = get over it. Could this be where we learned to say, "Just get over it."

Great, so now you're helpless, facing abandonment, change, and your fear of consequences when a nurse says, "Enough bonding and grieving." It's time to be cleaned up, fed (they always assume you're hungry) put in a clear plastic bed to sleep, and to be seen now by all: "Which one is it?" "Oh there he or she is, how cute." (Again, not at your best).

So I guess this is where our first belief about having to be presentable to the world comes from. Not just from our mothers and fathers saying later on, "Don't go out wearing dirty underwear. You might have an accident, and you don't want the doctor to see you in dirty underwear, do you?" (As if the doctor hasn't already seen us covered in muck, as we were pushed out by Mom into his or her arms.) Oh yes, it might not be the same doctor, so we must have on clean underwear. Somewhere our parents got the silly idea that we liked wearing dirty underwear. Maybe it was our attempt to control our world, or it could just have been spite. Yes, it must have been spite. This is when life starts to create conflicts and power struggles over the changes taking place in our lives.

Heading Home

Now it's time to go home for the very first time. You're all dressed up in a spiffy new outfit (it's all about appearances again) and you actually have somewhere to go. Hurray! If you're a girl you are probably wearing something distinctly feminine and pink. If you are a boy you're probably all decked out in masculine blue. Even though you are too young to understand the implications, this is your first encounter with the issue of gender identity and the way society automatically assigns different roles for boys and girls. Subtle as it may be, it is also the first time you are openly victimized by covert sexual abuse, which we will cover in much greater detail later in the book.

As you leave the sterile, monochromatic confines of the hospital you excitedly think, "Wow, my first entrance into a new world and my first ride in a machine (called a car)!" On the way home, the fresh air, low purring of the engine and the gentle vibration immediately put you to sleep as you yawn, "I could get used to this." Now mind you, not many people are in a pleasant mood when they're awakened abruptly before completing their full nap. So when the car suddenly stops and your proud parents hop out, you naturally get startled and upset and react, "Here we go again...What's going to happen now?" (fear, panic) So you cry, just to let them know, "HELP, I'm scared. Comfort me and tell me it's going to be all right." But no, they don't understand your messages yet, and you don't understand anything at all — except crisis, abandonment, fear, change, distrust, and panic.

Instead your crying makes them think you're hungry or wet or worse, the smelly one. Having checked out two of the three probable causes and finding no "evidence", they surmise it must be hunger. So they feed you (another food message?). That's when you slyly realize, "Not bad, cry and get fed, plus it stops the fear and thoughts of abandonment." You even begin feeling that maybe you can trust these people. Then comes the big burp and uh oh, you appear to have messed up your nifty new (sexually color-coded) outfit. Your mom and dad don't look too happy either because they wanted to take some pictures of their brand new baby's arrival home — just one more thing that's wrong with you.

Oh well, moving on now. Here come the ooh's and ah's from all the people you will learn more about later on. Surprise, surprise these large ogling strangers turn out in some way to be relatives or friends of your parents and you're the center of all that excited attention. Again, you are confused by a series of messages you cannot possibly begin to understand. That's when you wonder, "What have I gotten myself into, and how can I get out of it?" These are our first thoughts of abandoning our own family or leaving home, if you will.

Now that your first thoughts of leaving home have occurred, life continues on in a series of throw ups and dirty diapers, ups and downs at night, along with your mom and dad's inevitable mood swings. Their inconsistent behavior gives rise to new doubts and you think, "Perhaps I don't trust these people after all and they have control of my life! What's more, they don't seem to trust me very much." So you conclude it's time to take matters into your own hands and venture out.

Crawling seems like a good idea plus you decide you'll attempt a few sounds. This makes everyone excited and they mouth more of those strange sounds back that confuse you. Oh well, you're now OK since you are impressing them. But then they get frustrated that your sounds are not like their sounds (the first sign we must conform or we're not OK). So you try harder and soon you're able to get back in their good graces.

Challenges, Risks and Rewards, Acceptance and Approval

Next, after some prodding, you decide to take the next step towards acceptance by seeking unconditional love and approval. With your mom holding your hands at one end of the room and your dad at the other, enthusiastically clapping his encouragement, you take a risk and boldly attempt one, two, three, four steps and oops, you didn't make it. You fell before you got there.   Thank goodness for padding. Nevertheless, they're happy and excited but you're not really sure why. They're happy and you couldn't even trust them to catch you. So now you'll have to go it on your own again, alone again naturally (which by the way is the title of a great old song by Gilbert O'Sullivan; the guy knew what he was singing about).

What is this word NO, NO, NO?

You know by the tone of their voice it's not good so you ask, "Now what's wrong with me?" But when they say yes and clap their hands you know you're OK and you can't have your parents telling you no all the time. You want them to say, "YES, YES, YES".   Now you and I know that these messages, when left to interpretation, mean authority is to be tested and defied. You'll show them. So you figure, "We can have a tug of war over anything and everything off and on for the rest of our lives." You have now discovered the way to a great relationship is to have an ongoing power struggle. All will be well as long as you participate, even if you get tired of the game. You must keep playing because that's how we have all learned to interact with each other, and if one of the individuals involved makes a change it will affect everybody. Then there will be no more threats of abandonment, and they truly will abandon you once and for all.

Let's take a look at how the abandonment wounds would play out in the life of two people, Wendy and Jack. Let's see how Wendy and Jack's lives are played out as a result of their wounds that occurred for them growing up in dysfunctional family system. Wendy's painfully dysfunctional family system is obvious to the outside world, where as Jack's dysfunctional family system looks good to the outside world, but is dysfunctional on the inside. In Wendy's family, everyone outside the system knows something is wrong with them, but the family internally tries to maintain their denial by attempting to cover up and pretend everything is okay. In Jack's family, even though they don't appear dysfunctional to the outside world, internally they feel the pain and deny the dysfunction by shutting down and not talking about it, thus implementing the No Talk rule, inside or outside the family.

ON A CAUTIONARY NOTE – The remainder of this book is not for the faint of heart. However, it can help you identify a very common problem that many people suffer from and lead to a very real solution. This can make a big difference in your own life and subsequently, you can pass these benefits onto others by breaking the cycle for generations to come. After all, your emotional legacy to your children and grandchildren should be one of happiness and hope, not grief and pain. So I implore you to endure the often painful process of self-examination, self-discovery and self-healing. Not just so you can finally achieve happiness and fulfillment by breaking this vicious cycle but also in order to spare them from having to go through the same thing.

Wendy and Jack's story might be similar to how you were brought up, or their family's story may be similar to how you were brought up and live today. With that will come emotions and feelings of your own awareness of your own abandonment wounds, and life is much like an onion, peeling away the layers of the wounds. I hope this book, these stories, will enlighten you and help you heal the wounds, and peel away the layers of the onion, in helping you develop new and healthy relationships, and create your missing peace that you have been looking for so hard. For it is through the pain, that forgiveness and healing can occur. If at any point in the pages of this book you begin to feel emotional pain, please seek professional help and guidance on your journey of healing.

It might help you to begin to keep a journal of your emotions and feelings as you read through the pages of this book. If this exercise gets overly complicated, emotional or confusing for you, which commonly occurs when people are first introduced to these introspective, revealing concepts about highly personal issues, please re-read the interactions in Wendy's story over and over. You will begin to identify with them and see how your role-playing life may have taken on a life of its own. You may come to realize that somewhere along the line, you were left behind — abandoned by YOURSELF in order to protect yourself from the fear, panic and deep, deep pain of abandonment wounds.

******

This process of self-analysis often leads to the realization, "I am living for others and not for myself," along with the question, "Is this the life I really would have wanted had I been truly free to choose my role and my path?" It frequently causes a stinging pain brought about by a revelation over how much time one has lost living for others rather than for one's self. It also stirs thoughts of mortality and issues with mortality that propel many people to search for spirituality and the meaning of life. We are still seeking our missing piece by exploring a new religion, seeking 12-step support groups, and more, rather than knowing that our peace is within rather than without. When I know my peace is within, I can then seek support without to strengthen my inner peace through religion, 12-step support groups, and therapy.

Only when you get to the end of this initial phase of self-discovery and find no comfort in the external will you go within to experience the aching hurt of the many, many losses in your life so you can truly grieve. None of this will occur until you fully surrender and embrace the desire to experience a break in tolerance that says, "I'm lost. I am in pain, and I want it to stop!" Only then can you hope that, by breaking the tolerance level of your emotions, you will be motivated enough to change.

It is through the grieving process that you can move forward by overcoming your fear of change and consequences, so you can make the adjustments in your life needed to attain what you really want. With this break in tolerance, by becoming aware of the limitations you have set for yourself and by taking responsibility, you will be able to begin operating out of want instead of need. Once this occurs, you will set yourself up to become free — once and for all — a total acceptance of self, thus enabling you to love others without reservation and be loved in return.

******

So let us begin with family number one, the family whose dysfunctionality is obvious to everyone else despite their attempts to appear OK in order to help maintain their own defensive denial. So the narration of Wendy's life begins.

Chapter 2

Wendy's Story:

By Age Eight or Ten, We Know Right from Wrong- Wendy was no exception

By the time Wendy reaches 8 or 10, maybe even earlier due to the severity of the dysfunction in her family, she becomes unconsciously and emotionally more aware that she has a missing piece, and will begin to try and fill the hole at an even younger age than did her mom and dad. How she might attempt to fill her hole, since it's not safe to bring friends home, is by going to her friend's home. She also might not have many friends as she will isolate to hide the family secrets to the outside world — secrets like I don't have time to participate in any sports, games, social events at school because I have to go home to cook, clean, and take care of my younger brother. If overt or covert incest is going on in this home (which covert definitely is), Wendy doesn't want her friends subjected to it and possibly become aware of it, so she would prefer to go to her friend's home because it becomes perfect and supportive of her and her friend. She begins to dream: if only my family could be like that since her family is so obviously dysfunctional. However, she neglects to see that her friend's family has other dysfunctions.

On one brief occasion, when her friend does see her family dysfunction and sees the craziness, she says to Wendy, "I don't know how you can live like this." Since her friend is also in denial of her own family's dysfunction and has built a tolerance to it, she sees Wendy's family as even crazier and goes home to tell her parents, "I'm glad you are not like Wendy's parents." So in reality, Wendy and her friend are joined with the same goal in life: to look for their missing piece.

Wendy's hole gets bigger and bigger, so she asks for the thing she thinks will fill that hole and give her the unconditional love she so badly needs. Wendy wants a puppy or a kitten for Christmas. Mom and Dad have both been down this road themselves as kids and know the money and work involved with a pet, so they may do one of three things. First is to tell Wendy if we get you a pet (notice there are hints already appreciate us). Since there is no Santa Clause, only Mom and Dad, he comes with strings. (I often wonder if this is where the beliefs that men do the giving of gifts and women do the receiving come from, since Santa is always the male. Even in a family where the female may be the bread winner, Santa is still male. Just a thought.)

So they warn Wendy she has to be responsible for it. She will need to spend her allowance if there is one. Most likely there is not one in Wendy's family. So Wendy might have to figure out how that can happen. Then there is the taking care of the pet. Now Wendy has to rethink this. After all, with all she has to do in this family, does she really want to take on more? (What are any of us willing to pay for unconditional love that we think we will get from a pet?) Wendy also discovers that there is a price to be paid for her missing piece. (No more free lunches is re-enforced once again.) But because the hole is so deep and painful, she agrees and finally her missing piece arrives on Christmas morning. (How ironic that missing pieces often arrive in the way of gifts presented to us at Christmas, when the only one that can fill the missing piece is one's conscious contact with the spirituality of God within ourselves, which is the very reason this day was supposed to represent: honoring Him on his birthday.) We get focused on the material, rather than the spiritual. That's the reason we think there is something out there that is our missing piece, rather than our missing peace.

Wendy tried to fill her missing piece with the gifts from Mom and Dad, falsely believing that those gifts represent unconditional love that she so desperately needs and wants from them. (Denial– denial everywhere and not a drop to drink.)

The second option for the family might be to just tell Wendy NO. Wendy will now learn the hard lesson that in this family the only way she can get her missing piece is to grow up as quickly as possible and get out.   So she begins to deny her hole and internalizes the pain when it arises and waits for the day she can escape. Wendy might also get involved with boys at a younger age and begin to mistake physical advances as love and experiment with sex, alcohol, shopping, eating, etc.   She romanticizes everything in a relationship and when it ends, and it will end, she is devastated and it reinforces the *belief I'm on my own, and the only way I cannot hurt or get hurt is to shut down.* So she shuts down emotionally until the time she can escape.

The third options for Mom and Dad is to give Wendy a stuffed animal as a substitute, which even though Wendy is disappointed, she deludes herself by saying *they really wanted me to have what I wanted and they at least tried.* So she hangs on to the small bone (or crumb, if you will). This is where most of us learn to settle for crumbs in our lives. So Wendy begins her life long collection of stuffed animals or things, with the false belief that by hugging something like a stuffed animal will be enough to fill her missing piece till the right person comes along (which never does, not without strings anyway), reinforcing more work for Wendy. Now, she will grow up basing her worth on things she has in her life which are crumbs. She might become a compulsive shopper, of if she can't afford things, she will dream and fantasize about having them one day just as she did as a child. She might also develop envy or jealousy towards others for being able to have them. She will express those feelings by saying things like, "I would never do what Sheila had to do to get all the things she has. I would never just marry someone because they are rich. She really didn't love him. I know she's not happy." None of that in reality might be true. It's just Wendy's way to continue to cover up her issues of abandonment wounds and her missing piece.

The only way all of this could have been made functional to begin with, was to have parents that were role models that had a spiritual connection to God. When our parents have no missing piece and model it, it can't help but be passed down from generation to generation. This is why healing abandonment wounds is so important for breaking the cycle.

Free at last!

Her Declaration of Independence

After the teen years of abandonment and rejection from family and peers (what a painful mess that was), come the college years. What a great adventure! Play without prying family eyes and no word games to worry about — except for surprise visits and phone calls (when she can lie up a storm and ask for money). Yes, freedom at last! No more no, no, no /yes, yes, yes, right/wrong, protected sex/unprotected sex power struggles. It's finally over and she is finally allowed to take care of herself, which her mom and dad seem surprised she can do. (She doesn't know why; she's been doing it for years.) Of course there are one or two professors who are a lot like them, but she has learned to work around that.

Then she commits the ultimate defiance act of all time. She has either decided to get a job instead of going to college or has quit college to get a job, and her parents are NOT happy about it. But all the while she's never given up the search for her missing piece. She thought she had found it a few times in high school and almost married one once. Thank heaven she didn't, because the one she ended up with is even more perfect and that is the sweetest revenge.

Now having grown up with these people all her life, she knows that even though they say they are proud of her, there is always that unspoken word left hanging over her head 'but'. You could of, should of, would of are always on the tip of her mom and dad's tongues. If she is lucky (or unlucky, depending on your point of view) she now knows that whatever she does, it is not good enough and that makes her feel not good enough. But of course, they are proud of her, and she is saying to herself, "Sure they are."

The clock is ticking

What's that sound? Tick, tock. It's her biological clock. Panic, anger, resentment, fear, frustration . . . her pure rage that every time she has a conversation with her mom and dad it includes, "I hope you will give me some grandchildren before I die." Threats, threats, and always about them. What do they think, that she can produce someone out of thin air? Plus her attempts to rewind the clock just aren't working. She is in a struggle with Father Time. Well, at least it's not with her mother and father, or is it? As if it's not enough that they want grandkids, they also keep asking her, "What are you going to do with the rest of your life?" So she looks for the nearest job and/or the first person that says the magical words, "I love you. Will you marry me?"

Wow, true love, and he's a lot like her mom too (what a bonus). She has finally made it, even though she's not quite sure what she has made. But still, it feels like kismet. She is at a party and across the hazy room there he is, Mr. Wonderful. (Is it haze or the booze she's been drinking?) She knows this is the one for her. He fits everything on her list of things her parents are not and what do you know? She's everything his parents are not. What a wonderful match: heaven-made. They date. Have some problems. (Don't most? But that's OK.) They're in love and once they're married, things will change. (Will they ever.)

Now they decide that they're the perfect partners and the tick tock is getting louder, so the young couple moves in together or gets married. "Yeah that's it," she thinks, "It will really tick Mom and Dad off. Make them pay through the nose for all the past problems. Make them foot the bill for a big wedding then tell them, 'By the way, I might be pregnant.' What pay back! Now we'll see how bad they want grandchildren and see how fast a wedding date can be set and planned."

Romance, marriage, kids, and all the rest

The honeymoon is OK, not what she read in books but OK. Now they are back home and getting into the carousel of day-to-day life, which seems never ending. When the same old problems start to surface she thinks, "Heavens, have I made a mistake? Am I going to have to live with this person for the rest of my life? Every day he becomes more and more like someone I don't know (wait) or is it someone I know all too well–Mom? No, Dad? No, both! Good grief, I have married my mother and father, and we're beginning to have a relationship just like theirs. I must have a jinx on me."

Everywhere she looks, friends, co-workers and bosses are all a blur and she's back to the beginning again. What a cycle! If it weren't for her kids — who she has had each year attempting to get unconditional love that she doesn't get from her husband, family, and friends or at work — she's not sure she could bear it.

Now even the kids are not unconditional. They constantly want bottles; their diapers need to be changed all the time, and oh, the sleepless nights, fights over homework, car pool duty, basketball practice, dance lessons and on and on and on. She complains, "What more do they want from me? Where did I go wrong? Where did my LIFE go?" In addition, she knows that her husband is asking the same questions of himself. He has no time for her any more, and their sex life is barely lukewarm. She worries, "What if he leaves? Leaves me with all this mess. What will I do? My world is falling apart!"

When we fall apart we seek help

And that is exactly what Wendy did. She thought, therapy will fix it.

No, that has made it worse and better at the same time. At least she now has a place to go each week where she can vent and hear back the truth that ALL her problems stem from her layers of developing her layer upon layer of abandonment wounds. Then one day, when she is sick and tired of being sick and tired, someone says a few words that send panic and stark fear down her spine, because she knows they have hit the nail on the head and finally, she must face the pain and walk through it. These words can bring relief and pain at the same time. The words she hears are **self-abandonment**, **abandonment wounds**, and **transformation**.   So surrendering her guilt and shame and abandoning the *No-Talk* rule, Wendy seeks help.

And with that, her therapist Dianne asks her to begin her story of how her parents met.

Wendy: My dad, John, met his buddies at a local pick-up bar for their usual Friday night get-together and to get lucky, I guess. He was drawn to a table of laughing women across the room and saw, in his own words, the most attractive female he had seen in years. He became distracted by her and found it increasingly difficult to focus on sports and job talk.

While out for a night on the town to celebrate one of her friend's assumed-to-be exciting, new career as an airline flight attendant, my mom says she felt piercing eyes staring at her through the haze of the smoke-filled room. Having had a few drinks, which seemed to have heightened and alerted her senses, she knew then and there something major and wonderful was about to happen in her life– something that would create a great, rewarding change. (Isn't it grand how booze, a dimly lit room, and smoky haze can suddenly turn one's thoughts to romance?)

My mom, her name is Mary, spotted a red neon sign that flashed RESTROOM right over my Dad's left shoulder. Taking a chance and seizing the opportunity, my mom headed for the restroom door. Of course, she would have to walk close by Mr. Hunk on the way. "Oh, I'm so clumsy. Did I spill your drink?" she asked my Dad and reached for a napkin to wipe off his sleeve while his buddies poked each other in the ribs. He had already been attracted to her, and quickly replied, "No problem . . . may I buy you a drink?" My mom said yes, and the red restroom light faded into the dark never to be seen again.

As the evening went on, they exchanged phone numbers, planned to go out on a date and for the next few months a more perfect couple could not be found. Sure, a few red flags go up for my mom when they had some minor fights and arguments occurred, but she didn't read much into it. I know they broke-up briefly, but my mom thought he was still Mr. Right. She's told me once that he was everything her family wasn't. What more could she ask for? As to my Dad, he always complained that my mom was not easy to deal with.   That even before getting married, she would fly off the handle. He has always complained to me.

Dianne: He might have thought along the lines of.... "She's not as simple to deal with as I expected but how exciting — more emotion in one weekend than in an entire lifetime with my family. Mom and Dad probably won't approve of her, and she flies off the handle when I'm late or out with the guys, but the make-up sex is great. I think I could spend the rest of my life with her, maybe even start a family . . . plus she'll come around once we're married."

Your mom might have thought, "Yeah, he has a few problems. He's always late and he will not give up his night out with the guys. But at least he doesn't go into rages and break things. He has never hit me and after an argument, the make-up sex is really good. I could spend the rest of my life with a guy like this. Maybe even start a family with him, and of course, he'll come around once we're married."

Are you aware that your mother was covertly sexually abusing you by transgressing her boundaries and making you her confidant and sharing with you intimate details of her and your father's marriage? What you learned from this covert sexual abuse is a lack of boundaries and knowing what is appropriate or inappropriate in relationships with others, male or female. Were you aware that this covert sexual abuse by your mother has affected your sexuality in relationships with the opposite sex in your life and how you interact with them?

Wendy's eyes open widely and she responds after a pause.

Wendy: No, not really. This is what she would talk about, my Dad. How he didn't show her that he loved her. It was always about her. Anyway, on Valentine's Day, ring in hand, my dad asks my mom to marry him.

The honeymoon was OK. Not mind blowing, but an OK time. The weather was good, the hotel was gorgeous, and there were lots of things to do. They had a few arguments but nothing major, and soon they returned to get on with their "real lives" like my mom would say. (There was a long pause). My mom would always be angry at my dad and my dad was passive, I guess.

Dianne: Yes, we fall into the trap of thinking he'll change or she'll change and before long they do. Some small disagreements come up, but he won't fight. So they make a non-verbal deal, a secret pact, if you will. She will do all the feeling and he will do all the thinking.

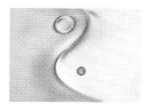

He thinks and she feels.
What a perfect balance.
They have each found their missing piece.
They are thinking that the two together,
make the perfect whole. Unfortunately,
neither has found their missing peace.

Dianne: As the routine of day-to-day life sets in and daily problems start to happen more frequently, the more promotions and outside demands that occur, the more distance that begins to build between them. Your mom may have grown fearful of your dad threatening to leave, if she did not support him completely, and he began to become her total focus in life. Support at any cost.

Let's visualize how your family system might look in a classic role-playing exercise. Imagine if you will, Mary sitting in a chair facing Jack. She has to sit in a chair because she's exhausted doing all her jobs as the designated "feeler" and John's one-woman support system. She must remain totally focused on him, so that he won't abandon her. John is standing facing away from Mary, as he is not really there. He is focused on the 'what ifs' and what could have been. One of his hands is in a fist on top of Mary's head, and his body is twisted awkwardly in the opposite direction heading for the door. John's other arm is pointing away, as if he is trying to grasp something just out of reach beyond the door. This demonstrates his preoccupation with looking for the missing piece in his life that marriage didn't fill — the gaping hole in the pit of his stomach. It's not that he doesn't love or care for her, but there's got to be more to life than this. How can he have his cake and eat it too? (Evidently, he has forgotten there are no more free lunches.) Still, his underlying fear is that if she finds out any of this, *she* will abandon *him*.

Wendy's obvious dysfunctional family

While Mary feels exhausted having to have all the feelings (and boy, are there a lot of them), her biggest fear of all is, "What if he abandons me?" She begins to get into self-absorption as well and thinks, "Why me? My needs are on hold. When is it going to be my turn?" Her hand then goes up to rest on her forehead in what is known as the Co-Dependent Salute or, if you will, "Poor me, this is giving me a headache."

As John begins to focus outside the marriage on whatever (work, sports, nights out with the guys — and we know what Mary's fear is there, after all, that's how they met), a lot of their arguments begin to focus on all the issues EXCEPT the most important ones. The ones they should be talking about are emotional distancing, mental and physical drifting apart, and their mutual fear that if they confront what is really going on, one of them will leave.

One of their typical arguments might have been something like this: Mary accuses, "You're never home. You care more about your friends than me, and you've become so self-centered." Jack defensively snaps back, "You nag too much. If you had a life of your own you wouldn't be so focused on mine. You're the one who has become self-centered, and you've been reading too many of those damn romance novels and self-help books."

Furthermore, both of your parents have now begun their own search for their missing piece, as the marriage is no longer working to fill the hole. It's like the band-aid has been ripped off and ouch it hurts. In looking for a pain reliever, they grab a hold of the reason they wanted to be together in the first place, which was to have a family. But not just any family — the perfect family.

That's when they decide this would be a good time to start. After all, they both need a distraction. So they decide to have a child. If a couple like this cannot have a child of their own, they may adopt or even substitute a pet for it. It's at these times in relationships, that couples look to children as a life jacket to save the sinking ship of their marriage to avoid abandonment, which is what your parents did when they decided to have you and your brother. You, becoming the hero as you were the first born in your family, learned to be the family's competent, strength, and perfectionist face to the outside world. Thus, your job was to protect the family by looking good at all costs. How stressful has that been for you?

Distractions come in all shapes and sizes

While attempting to start a family, more distance grows between them. John begins to focus more and more on looking outward. If an addiction has developed or is beginning to develop, he medicates his pain by increased use of the substance, or he might even add a new one. If at first he used alcohol to deaden the pain, he might also begin using cocaine, affairs, and gambling. Simultaneously, Mary medicates her pain by becoming more and more focused on John. Her main mission in life at this point is to get pregnant. She is driven by the fear that if she does not hurry up and conceive she might lose him. There is nothing more painful or lonely than to be alone in a relationship. In fact it is less lonely to just be alone.

Dianne: Now let me explain the reasons Jack's fist was on Mary's head in the previous description of role-playing. In reality his fist represents several different things. First, it not only represents dominance but also displaced aggression that he really feels toward himself, which he has displaced onto her.

Secondly, it represents dependency. Without her support, he would not be able to stand on his own. He would be unable to endure his fear and pain. He needs her to serve this thankless, supportive function and is afraid that if she leaves, he won't be able to make it without her. If she were to leave, he would have to go back to the bars to find someone else right away, and he might already secretly have someone in mind or even lined up "just in case". Deep inside he knows what is happening and so does she, therefore their Dance of Denial must continue to hold it together.

Next, Mary's other arm comes up to support Jack's (the arm with a fist on her head) in an attempt to keep some control. It is her way of supporting him while becoming a master in the art of manipulation. She must try to manipulate his world, her world, and anyone else's world that will let her exercise a degree of control. If she develops an addiction (be it alcohol, drugs, sexual addiction, sexual anorexia, shopping, gambling, an eating disorder or something else), it serves as a distraction until the "real" solution (a family) comes along. Her whole focus is to manipulate, in an attempt to gain control. This is commonly done in several ways including guilt trips, arguments over anything except the real problems, the silent treatment, sexual withdrawal, etc. Concurrently, she also becomes adept at the art of covering up any consequences John may suffer. She might call his boss to say he is sick when in fact he is not (maybe he's just hung over that day). She might also begin telling lies about what is really going on to friends, family, and neighbors.

All of this pressure takes its toll on both of them. John becomes more and more caught-up in the denial that his addiction (which could by now have become a physical one) is actually a substitute for his missing piece. Meanwhile, Mary equates control with avoidance of abandonment and begins operating totally out of fear–a fear that is derived from the fact that she cannot control everything. By trying to control John, she's attempting to avoid his abandonment of her. If manipulation and control can give her just five or ten minutes of comfort in a day, she's going to do it. She rationalizes this by saying, "I can't be happy unless you are happy, so damn it, get happy!" She will do whatever she has to do to make that happen because to her, just a few minutes of peace and some restful sleep have become like gold. She is very tired.

Before we proceed with our increasingly grim "family portrait," it is important to mention that highly dysfunctional relationships like this are always based on the fact that both partners live in constant fear of abandonment. As a result, they are always tense, on edge, expecting the worst, causing the body to tense up and begin to create its own memories. Thus, individuals that come from this type of family system will develop muscle stiffness or stress knots in their bodies. They are often referred to as body memories and through the healing process of the letting go of the abandonment wounds often these body memories will be released.

I personally believe that people do not wind up in an abusive relationship solely as the result of playing-out their chosen childhood roles. They must learn this kind of victimization from their family of origin. To those observing from the outside it is incomprehensible that someone would tolerate so much emotional, mental, verbal, and possibly physical abuse. Even more incomprehensible is that many parents in a dysfunctional family like John and Mary's watch silently as their own children are being abused by their spouse–sometimes for many, many years on end. This is very common because they are in deep denial and until their tolerance levels for emotional pain is broken, things will not change. In fact, they will progressively get worse.

It is my belief that the unhealthy behavior patterns, which develop around avoidance and denial stemming from issues of abandonment, are the leading cause of death in the world today. If you look at the leading causes of death in the United States alone, they are all stress-related diseases. Even accidental death can fall under this category, because accidents are often the result of preoccupation with what is going on in one's life versus being focused on the here and now. For example, if a person is constantly distracted with thoughts like, "How am I going to tell her about . . . ?" or "How can I maintain control of him when he seems too distant or indifferent?" or "How am I going to make this nightmare go away?" (everything except what they are doing at the moment), accidents can occur and death can follow.

So, returning to our story of fairytale romance gone wrong . . . the bottom line here is that both John and Mary are terrified of abandonment. By staying together each is able to know who they are, at least as far as their relationship to each other goes. If she stepped away from him or if he stepped away from her, each would feel like they ceased to exist. In that case, each of them would either realize they have a serious problem and get into a recovery program, or more likely find someone else equally flawed and end up right back in another unhealthy relationship. If so, the next relationship will be even worse, because they simply no longer know how to function without a crisis to focus on.

If either John or Mary should find someone else, their new partner or mate would appear at first to be more functional than the last one or even the opposite. After all, they would not want to make the same mistake again. However, their individual, yet unacknowledged search for their own missing piece is more desperate now and like most diseases, it is progressive in nature. In fact, they often choose someone worse than their last partner. So this becomes a dance they both do together because neither one of them could do it alone.

The point of this really is: he is not making her do this, and she is not making him do this. They are just coping with each other's need to avoid abandonment out of fear of their own loss of identity, spirituality, and the need for unconditional love. Thus, we are right back to the mutual support of each other's self-abandonment. Still this is the only way they can keep their co-dependent support system in place until the true distraction (a child) comes along.   John plays on Mary's low self-esteem pushing her fear-of-abandonment buttons. They each act as if it is the other one's fault in order to maintain their rationale while continuing to look for their own missing piece.

It should also be noted that there is no difference between adopting a pet, starting an avid hobby, taking on more projects at work, starting a business of your own, having affairs, frequenting strip clubs, seeking prostitutes, becoming a prostitute, watching internet porn, online gaming or shopping, or disordered eating when seeking a distraction from the core issue of abandonment wounds. These and many other things can serve the same purpose prior to thinking about adopting or having a child. However, when the attempt to add the distraction of a pet, hobby, or affair or any of the above listed does not work (which it will not), a couple like John and Mary will have a child, or they will adopt. This is occurring in today's world more and more frequently than in past generations. Even singles (both male and female) in increasing numbers are adopting children. The loss of one's spirituality, identity, attachment and detachment, and multiple addictions stem from the core beginnings of abandonment wounds which are reaching epidemic proportions.

Now let's think about the long-term effects of stress as it relates to our unhappy couple

Being put in these awkward, uncomfortable mental and emotional positions for sometimes five, ten, fifteen, twenty years at a time or more, and always having to hold that position in order to maintain the (dysfunctional) status quo, becomes so painful and stressful that physical problems begin to occur. John may develop medical problems as a result of his addictions, like liver disease or pancreatitis associated with alcoholism, heart problems resulting from high stress or even obesity from an eating disorder as it often causes the weakening of various body parts due to increased pressure from the extra weight. Mary may have exactly the same problem as the result of developing psychosomatic illnesses that are just as real like headaches, backaches, and stiff muscles. Her mind and emotional responses directly affect the organs of the body vs. his being the consequence of addictions. Either way, they both suffer very real medical problems that will need to be treated. Because they can now attribute their problems to physical ailments instead of the spiritual ailment of spiritual bankruptcy they both feel as a result of their abandonment wounds, they can continue the denial that their relationship has problems and is not filling what they consider to be their missing piece.

To further illustrate how these dynamics work in a relationship, let's return to our roleplaying illustration of Wendy's family poses. If you had to hold Mary's pose (with her arm supporting Jack's, while his fist is pushing down on her head and her other arm constantly being held up to her forehead) for weeks, months, or even years, you might not feel so good. Imagine if you had to constantly push a fist down on someone's head while twisting to turn away with one arm outstretched in the opposite direction for all that time. You might not feel too good either.

The central issue is that John and Mary are surrounded by mounting stress. So in order to survive, they develop a higher and higher tolerance level for pain, until they neither react nor even notice the stress. As a matter of fact, they begin under-reacting to major stresses and overreacting to minor stress.

So now let the real distraction begin!

Enter The Super Hero and Marriage Saver, Wendy (Wendy has been born)

After a pregnancy befitting a dysfunctional relationship like this, as seen in the beginning, John and Mary's first-born is a girl named Wendy who soon learns that she is the adult here. To illustrate this added dynamic or dimension to our already struggling, emotionally crippled family, let's return to our role-playing for a moment. Wendy bears the burden to face the world while she is trying to hide the dysfunction going on at home. This is stressful for a child trying to be take on an adult role in the family system.

Dianne: First, I want you to use your imagination again and remember the poses our couple has been holding all this time. Mary (now a mom) is still sitting in a chair exhausted, supporting John's arm with his fist on her head, while doing the Codependent Salute. Our new dad is still preoccupied with his body turned away from her and his other arm is still outstretched seeking fulfillment elsewhere. Then they put you Wendy, their new daughter, standing in front of them, facing outward with your back to both of them. You have one arm bent back to support your mother's elbow (on Mary's "salute" arm). Your other arm is stretched out in front of your father, as if trying to protect him from the world, his addiction, and himself. You do this in the hope of keeping him from making a fool of or hurting himself or others, and you want to keep other people from finding out what it's really like to have to live in this troubled family.

Wendy: I didn't do it deliberately....consciously. I just did what I felt I had to do. I was   a kid. I didn't know better. Look at me now. I still don't know. How could I have been put in this situation? I wasn't born for this crap. I'm more than that!

Her body begins to tense up. She feels as if a veil is starting to lift slowly. It's overwhelming. Her eyes fill with regrets and undeclared surrender. Dianne remains silent for a few moments so that Wendy can feel the pain. When Wendy regains some composure, Dianne continues.

Dianne: Let us now examine our revised family portrait from your perspective Wendy. You were also in denial. You wanted to believe that the others didn't know what was going on (even though deep down you knew they knew something was wrong, but were not quite sure what). You might also have been trying to protect the outside world from your father's self-destructive behavior. For example, you might have hidden the car keys so he wouldn't drive drunk, or you might have stepped in and taken any physical abuse that he would otherwise have inflicted on your mother (or your brother after he came along). Please note that if incest is going to occur in this family, you as the first born daughter would most likely be the sexually abused child.

Tragically, in playing your role as a Super Hero /Over Achiever /or Adult Child, you would also keep your mouth shut to protect the family and keep it together at any cost — even if you had to be the recipient of more abuse. You learned to be tough. You became a survivor of all things. All the while you felt you had to maintain a great big smile to make others think that it really wasn't all that bad. "Everything is fine here". (Fine, meaning insecure, neurotic or an emotional wreck, as it relates to what clients in recovery programs really mean when they use that word to describe themselves.)

As a matter of fact it was imperative that you kept smiling and acting as if everything was okay. For if you didn't, you would have cried and that was not only dangerous in your family, but you were afraid that if you ever started crying you would never be able to stop. The whole time Wendy, you were smiling, though you felt shame, guilt, fear, confusion, and panic. You felt inadequate and had learned never to trust people. (If incest or covert sexual abuse is going on, you certainly won't trust men. You will always see them as the enemy and wanting things from you, and not give anything to you or the relationship. People like you, Wendy, often get trapped in relationships where your partners are needy, self-absorbed, and narcissistic.)

Either way, Wendy, as an Adult Child you made a firm commitment to yourself at a very early age that you would never, ever marry anyone like your parents. Your anger also began to build towards your mother even more than your father because of her inability to see what was going on and for not protecting you from your father's abuse. But most of all, you learned not to trust yourself.

Wendy begins to cry softly at first, but the tears keep pouring with each growing sob. She has to gasp for air as she fights for the words to say. Her first truth on the canvas of her new life that was being painted right before her eyes was her realization that her life had been about abuse, created by the abandonment wounds of her family system and dysfunction. She cried softly.

Wendy: I went through a lot growing up. I was so, so sad. I felt lost. I was so alone. No child deserves to feel alone. I couldn't bare it! I didn't deserve that. I didn't. It wasn't my fault. I just wanted to be loved.   And now, look how I live? Look at my marriage.   I knew I wanted things to be different.   But my marriage has been so much like my parent's marriage. (Her sobs become more intense. She has no energy to fill in her emotions with words. She braces herself and fixes her eyes down at the carpet. She becomes silent. There are no more tears to dry. All is quiet). My children. I'm not there for them. Am I doing the same thing to them? Am I not doing anything to stop this cycle? What can I do? Is there anything I can do? I don't want my children to go through this emptiness. What am I supposed to do? For my kids. For my marriage.

Dianne: What about for you? What can you do for yourself?
Now her education and journey towards the completion and
self-healing can begin at last.   Dianne asks Wendy if Jack
would be willing to share his story with her.   When Jack and
Dianne meet, John's story reveals itself.

Chapter 3

The Family that Looks Good Must be Good?

Jack's Story

Jack does come in to add more to the picture. Dianne asks him to begin his story of how his parents met.

Jack: I know my mom always starts with the story that they both sat in the singles group at their church. How they first caught each other's eye, but how she looked away. She didn't want to let my Dad know she was interested. It wasn't proper, she would explain to us, to be so forward, but she couldn't help but glance his way every few moments only to discover that he was looking back. Blushing and feeling somewhat exposed, she formulated her plan to meet him.

You see, she had had it drummed into her all her life that it's all about appearances. Coming back from the distraction and the unnerving eyes of my Dad, Chandler, my mom, Cindy, hears the leader in the church group talking about a singles weekend retreat that was coming up the following weekend. She thought that if she attended, he might be there and someone would introduce them. My mother noticed an acquaintance talking to my Dad.

Later, when my mom says her acquaintance spoke to her, she expressed her interest in going to the retreat. My mom has shared the story a million times. She included that she was hoping to rally those that might introduce her to the new guy, as well as hoping she would know someone there and wouldn't be left to meet new people on her own. She made arrangements to possibly ride up together to the retreat's location and soon eased the conversation into finding out how her acquaintance knew the new guy.

Dianne: Do you notice the word *acquaintance* came up several times when you were talking about your mom. Has it occurred to you that your mom is so afraid to get anyone close to her for fear: *if they really see (appearances) me for who I am, they won't like me.* Could that be one of your mother's abandonment wounds from her dysfunctional family system, so she has only acquaintances and no close friends? Does that remind you of your wife Wendy at all?

There is a pause. Jack looks confused and is more preoccupied with finishing the story.

Jack: Something I had not considered. As I was saying, my mom soon found out that his name was Chandler and he worked with her friend at the grocery store. They would take a break at the same time and that they were on the store's bowling team. He was a nice guy. In no time, she invited my mom to join the team. They needed a new member, and no one at work wanted to play. My mom thought that was her perfect opportunity so she signed on. She now had the day and time set up. All she had to do now was to show up. When she tells the story, she explains how when she said, "I just might do that," she was already planning in her mind what she was going to wear.

Dianne: Have you ever noticed how manipulative your mother is? She now knows Chandler's name, where he works, and what he does on Tuesday nights all without having to show her interest. When your Dad tells the story of how they met, what does he share?

Jack: He talks about how he did notice, but because she was focused on appearances and seemed to have been attending the meetings a while and to know a lot of the people, he would proceed with caution. He would wait to get the scoop about

Cindy. He had already found out her name. On Tuesday, when they were in a more social setting, he would find out the *scoop about the chic named Cindy*, were his exact words. Up to that Tuesday my mom made several trips to the supermarket with my Grandmother in hopes to see him and maybe her friend who worked with him could introduce her, and she could meet him sooner. The attraction was strong, and she wanted out of her home. Marriage was already in her mind.

The first few times in the store she got glimpses, but there were no opportunities to make contact. Once, right in the produce section, looking at the bananas which she doesn't even like, she catches a glimpse. He says, "Hi, I saw you at church the other night. "Yes, it was a good meeting that night. Sometimes they are not always that good." She just wanted to ask him if he was new in town, or better yet, what was his story and *let's get married.*

My dad thought she was cute, shy, ripe for the picking, and that she could be the one for him. He thought she was definitely a virgin and that he must go slowly. She had a look on her face that said, "I'm available." My Dad had been looking for the proper girl all his life and so the romance began. He asked, "Do you like to bowl?" My mom explained she had recently joined the store bowling league on Tuesday nights and asked if he liked to bowl. My mom went on to explain she had tried bowling once before and that it looked like fun. My dad was happy to hear that she had joined the league and added that he could give her a few pointers. So the very next Tuesday at 6 p.m. they meet again at the bowling alley. They meet, bowl a few games, and spend time together at the coffee shop in the bowling alley.

Jack goes on to share that the romance begins casually at first, but soon it becomes more intense and both are sure *this is the one.* He brings out the freedom for Cindy to express herself; she listens and understands Chandler. He is everything that is different from my family, and I'm sure that he is perfect—after all, his father is a preacher and his mother is a stay at home mom. They become exclusive and they have their first sexual experience; and he was right, she was a virgin. Realizing now that she saved herself for him, he is convinced that this is true love. She thinks this is what I have waited for all my life and I want out of my family and into one that gives me the freedom to do all the things I was never allowed to do before. Since they have become exclusive, they use sex as the expression of their love, occurring daily. (After all, both must make up for the love they both never got at home.) A few months go by and her period is late. Cindy becomes moody and fearful. Chandler doesn't understand the change, so he begins to ask if her feelings have begun to change. She says, "Oh no, they are stronger than ever." He pushes her for answers, and finally out of fear and panic, she confesses, "I'm late and afraid I'm pregnant." In spite of her fear of abandonment by him, rejection and shame she will inflict on her family, the shame at having to share that she has been sexually active, she convinces herself that she has wanted to have Chandler's baby since she first met him. Most of all, she wants to start her life as Mrs._. She tells Chandler. He says that it's sooner than what he had planned, but he loved her and wanted her to be the mother of their children. Both think, what more do we need? He/she loves me. We will have a family and live happily ever after (After all, isn't that what is supposed to happen when you love each other?) They decide to tell their families and the plans for their wedding begin.

Cindy's mother decides her Dad will not react well, so she decides not to tell him why the marriage should happen so soon - other than Cindy wants to honor her sister, (after all, she is her hero) and get married on her anniversary. She also decides that, even though she did not like her sister's wedding dress, it is an option. Her mother tells her they need to save all the money they can for the baby and since timing is important, Cindy decides to go along. Chandler is so happy that his dream is coming true that he will do whatever, just so they are married. Chandler's family, as always, is detached and glad he will be living in this new town away from his father's ministry. They are glad that everyone will be happy that the preacher's son has finally decided to give up his wild lifestyle and settle down with a respectable girl and have a family. The fact that she is pregnant is OK. It will make their son settle down faster, and since they live in another town, they can continue the facade that they have been saved and all is well. Cindy and Chandler buy that idea and don't care; after all, it is about love and the new baby. Cindy thinks finally, *I am loved forever.* Chandler thinks, *I have hit the Jack pot* (no pun intended) and *she loves me and will never leave.*

The night before the big day, Cindy and Chandler go to the church and find it open with no one in sight. They walk up to the altar and kneel, pledging their love towards each other. Cindy throws up and both are convinced that morning sickness has already started and Chandler fusses over her. Both become more convinced that this is true, deep, forever love. The next morning Cindy wakes to pain in her stomach and goes to the bathroom. She sees blood and is afraid she is losing the baby. What to do? There's panic, fear, pain, and grief. Fear that Chandler will leave her, and pain at the thought of losing her baby. (Notice she has already decided that this is her baby).

After talking and crying to her mother, she calms down and realizes that she has started her period. Mother tells her she can cancel the wedding. (Cindy's mother would love this. After all, when Cindy leaves there is no more covert abuse from Dad and Mother will have to deal with the distance that has grown over the years between her and Cindy's dad.) Cindy is thinking that she will lose the only person she will ever love and any hopes of having a baby. She insists that it would look bad for everyone if the wedding is canceled. All day up to her mother being escorted down the aisle by Chandler's best man, Cindy is told she can call it off. Dad becomes tearful and says, "My little girl is all grown up." Cindy did not have a chance to tell Chandler that she was not pregnant, and that she has started her period. (You must not see the groom on you wedding day. HA! It is bad luck). She has horrible cramps, and she wonders when the ibuprofen will kick in and whether or not she can walk down the aisle without pain and kneel all the way through the song "Ave Maria." Cindy takes her first step. She ignores her inner fears that this is not a good start and whether or not he will love her or feel trapped by her. She feared that he would hate her when he found out that she was not pregnant and that they would be starting their honeymoon while she was on period. Plus, the pressure was on. Chandler's parents, brothers, sister, plus half of his Dad's congratulation, were present. Cindy's parents, friends and families were too. Over three hundred and fifty people were waiting for the bride to walk down the aisle to her prince charming and live happily ever after.

The strong need to believe she was loved by Chandler pushes her forward and she takes the first steps down the long isle that seems like it would never end. She walks toward her true love and new life, (building layer upon layer of feelings of abandonment wounds on top of each other. This will create a repeat pattern effect, as we will always recreate the familiar - a comfortable and safe emotional place to be). Telling Chandler that first night in the Motel 6 causes Cindy fear. He will leave and say it is over (before it even gets started). She prays he will embrace her and share in her disappointment at not being with child - crying together, making their love stronger than ever. After all the tears and pain while telling Chandler and receiving no response, Cindy has him open the champagne. They toast and confess their undying love and that they will work on getting pregnant right away. Cindy begins to feel that true love has prevailed. Chandler on the other hand says, "Drink the champagne. Enjoy. I need a beer. I'll be back." Cindy drinks the whole bottle and falls asleep, crying because Jack doesn't return. At 2 a.m. Chandler comes in drunk and falls asleep. He wakes up at 10 a.m., takes a shower and says, "Let's go. We need to make it to California by tonight. We have reservations." Driving in silence and pretending to keep up the pretense that things are OK, both begin to ask themselves, "Why does this hurt so much?" and "Do I love him/her?"

The struggle now becomes how I can fix it or love conquers all. The one way to make Chandler realize he loves me, and it is up to me to make him want to change. Maybe if I was expecting, he will love me again, and we can live happily ever after as planned. So, the way they coped with their relationship was to follow the old tried and true rule--appearances and lots of love making. From the old saying, from one of the old wars, "all is well on the home front." How ironic. The reason to get married is for the recreation of the perfect family.

Cindy begins to believe that having their son worked. The relationship came together. They were both happy and proud to be parents of a beautiful bouncing boy named Jack. Chandler decides to turn his life around, and around is an understatement. Chandler becomes the small town minister (like his father) and Cindy becomes the loving and devoted wife and mother. Both are the upstanding role models in the local area and are active and upstanding community leaders.

As Jack tells Dianne the story of his parent's life together as he understood it to be, prior to his birth, Dianne begins to gather a picture of how these two, Wendy and Jack, had come together to work through their core family issues of abandonment wounds. Diane asked Jack to imagine Chandler, his father, standing with his back to his wife's Cindy with her back to him, so close but not touching.

Dianne: To the outside world they look like they are touching. (This is all about looks.) So, if you think they are close, that's good enough. They will feel more comfortable just knowing that you think they are close, because they don't want to risk the possibility of intimacy. They don't want to appear vulnerable to each other.

Another thing about being back to back is, because they are always pulling in opposite directions, they don't know how to work together. (This could show up in other areas of their life like difficulty with team work on other projects at   work.)   It is also showing some anger and blame towards each other, but primarily it is showing fear: *I don't want you to see my face. I don't what you to know who I am, because if you do, I'll be lost and I could be hurt.* Or maybe they have both already been hurt and are injecting the safe "No Talk rules" they grew up with to protect themselves from feelings of abandonment. So it's a game of pretense. *Let's pretend we are happy to the rest of the world,* but they will never connect emotionally. They don't talk about anything that will upset them. They talk about the weather, they talk about the neighbors. That's a lot of fun. Criticizing other people is an avoidance technique they employ to avoid seeing what is really going on in their family. So they continue to talk about other relatives, they talk about the news, they talk about the furniture in the house, but they never, never talk about anything of substance. Especially, they never ever talk about the hurt and pain that is going on in their relationship.

So now imagine them standing back to back and looking out at you, the observer, and smiling. Cindy's finger is pointing over her shoulder at Chandler, and Chandler has his back towards Cindy and his finger is pointing over his shoulder towards her in a blaming way. What they are saying is, everything is perfectly fine here. So you see, nothing is wrong. I'm not the guilty party.

Jack's looking good family

In the next session with Wendy, after gaining an insightful story of Jack's family history, she begins to pull it together for Wendy.

Dianne: You know there is a saying in the twelve step program that fits here. When someone tells you they are fine they are really saying is *I'm freaked out insecure, neurotic and an emotional wreak.* This does seem to be a good description of this looking good family. Both Cindy and Chandler, with their free hand, they are making a fist and keeping it down to their side, as if trying to hide it. It's a secret. What they are saying is *I'm angry, but I will not let anyone know it. I'm angry and I will not let you know directly, because if I do, you might leave and abandon me.* So they play this sarcastic game with each other especially around other people, in public (because one would never make a scene in public), and in front of their son Jack. When they are alone they are also passive aggressive with each other. When asked a question, one pretends not to hear, making the one asking the question to become frustrated. (Sort of like a dog wagging its tail and pissing on your foot at the same time.) However, the rule is, no one must see us fight.

In public their smiles look nice, but somewhere inside they begin to believe (maybe we really hate each other...maybe the love has died because Cindy now feels Chandler believes she lied and trapped him into marriage by telling him she was pregnant. That she then gets pregnant on the strained honeymoon, while other people think they are too good to be true. They are right. They are too good to be true.

They will also pull others into a triangulation. They will make a joke about each other to others, keeping others in the middle, listening to what appears to be comical satire banter, and yet they will not talk directly face to face with each other. They have a way of always needing a third party to communicate with each other, thus the term triangulation. This is where Jack was valuable to his mother Cindy and father Chandler. He became the one to blame and would be their mediator. These are things that would go on at home with family and close friends, but out in the community, it is always Sunday morning standing on the church steps: false front and appearance of the perfect family united together in closeness.

Others might envy and admire these very upstanding pillars of the community. Others don't base their opinions on the financial status of this family. Any looking good home is not based on rich, poor, middle class, heterosexual, or homosexual characteristics. It is based on the outward appearances which will always be the same: what a great family...they are so close and upstanding. They are secretly looked up to socially and they may be very visible in the community like Jack's family. They could be a minister, fireman, banker, politician, counselor, principals, or teachers. Something that people would say would be, "You know, he/she is a doctor, lawyer, etc. They are doing well." They are living externally the life of the Jones. They could be the Jones. They are a close family; they must be good people. Outwardly, Jack's family smiles, are nice to everyone, they always do the right thing that others expect from a healthy looking family. Often they will carry it to the extreme of having to wear the right clothes. Cindy, for example, won't go out of the house without make up or being presentable and never says the wrong thing. People generally find her supportive. The family will never, ever have any confrontations with each other or others in public. Even at home, in lieu of confrontation or disapproval, it is expressed through silence or avoidance.

Everyone assumes Jack's family, or any family like this, is the role model of a good, healthy family and the pillar of the community. As a matter of fact Wendy, your family might have said these things internally after meeting Jack's family, because saying it out loud would set off your Dad in a rage. After meeting Jack's family, they might internally have said, "If only we could be like them." At the same time they might have also thought, "But they are too good to be true." (And they were.)

Jack's father, Chandler, buries his head in work. Furthermore, this type of family might often get into being super critical of each other and participate in compulsive behaviors. This family believes, "If anything is worth doing, it is worth doing right," reinforcing the need for perfectionism and conforming, which created rebellious behaviors in your husband Jack. An example of this is his risky behaviors of being a dare devil in the beginning. Because you were so fearful of risk, he became irresistible to you. When Jack's family is in emotional pain, his family will medicate with compulsive behaviors. (If any of you out there can relate to Jack's family, you will be attracted to the Wendy's of the world and vice versa.)

The rules and rewards in the family come from what you do or how you look to others. Compulsive and rebellious behaviors are ignored as long as they are behind closed doors. John was also inspired by his rebellious behaviors. They set him up for *if you want to rebel, you must work extra hard to be the best at work,* making him a workaholic - a way of self-medicating the emotional pain of abandonment wounds. His mother might have become compulsive about the   home. She might have focused on its appearance. Everything has a place and must be in it. Her way to rebel is to withhold sex from Jack's father and blame Jack for problems in their marriage.   So what she originally believed would save her marriage, she now believes is the problem and the cause of their unhappiness. If Jack's father was a minister, lawyer, doctor, principal, psychologist, etc., he may be extremely admired and appreciated by the community and seen as the trusted one.

Outside of the family everyone says, "Why that Chandler, what a great guy. Why, he would give you the shirt off his back. What they didn't know was that at home he wouldn't even give them the time of day. He would find someone to give them what they wanted or needed and make it look like he did them a favor. When Jack's father came home, Jack said he was often sullen, depressed, and would go off from the family to read the paper, drink a beer, and park in front of the T.V till time for bed.

He may have retreated to his office to medicate his pains of isolation and   emotional detachment that had occurred in his relationship with his wife and son. He may have acted out to avoid these feelings through watching porn till time for bed or often-times falls asleep in front of his computer after masturbating himself to calm and relax him from a stressful day. Or, he may have a hobby that no one is allowed to participate in. He retreats to the garage where he works at his hobby till time for bed, often going to bed without saying good night to any of the family. He is the loner in the system. No wonder Jack wants your attention and anything that takes that away is seen as not worthy of his attention. When it is unavoidable, he leaves to find something or someone that will give it to him. Jack was getting double messages from his father: be perfect in public; withdraw, act out, and show no feelings at home.

Some of the other rules John lived by are important.   Notice Wendy that his family has unspoken, secretively enforced rules, where as your family's rules are often enforced sporadically, due to the inability to not be involved in the family system. The other important thing that Jack saw his family members as was "thinkers." *Think, be rational, be logical. You must do the right thing, don't embarrass the family.*

There is a belief that somewhere there is a book that exists that has all the right things in it. (Those of you that felt that when you picked up this book now realize some of your own family dynamics that caused you to pick up this book and buy it.) I often wonder where that book is...that got it right. Because when you go into a different home, their book does not match the one your family is using, so that shouldn't be the right book either. After all, Jack thinks your family is nuts and his is perfect. Am I right, Wendy?

Wendy becomes tearful. She has put all of this information together and is now exploring how both her childhood and Jack's childhood have affected each other and reinforced her fears of abandonment. She is also now beginning to see that it has not been all about her and her family's obvious dysfunction that is creating problems in her and Jack's relationship. It is also about his.

Dianne now meets with Wendy and Jack and continues talking to them about the effects of their family dynamics on their current relationships.

Dianne: Jack, your family knows what the right thing is. (They really do know and they know how to "think") That can and often is dangerous because it creates shutting down feelings. So armed with these rules, and not having to be emotionally attached, has been a way for you to avoid the loneliness you felt in your family. Detachment became your way Jack of protecting yourself to avoid the pain of the emotional neglect of your family. You also became a love avoidant, not able to develop intimacy in any relationship - not just the one you have with Wendy.

Wendy, since there was no intimacy expressed in his family or yours, the two of you are trying to get blood from a turnip by making each other you're missing piece. The problem with this, Wendy, is that neither one of you has the emotional availability to connect on an intimate level, so filling that void again is driving a wedge into your happiness. Both of you look outside of yourselves and your relationship, to fill that missing piece. Like in both of your families, you decided to have another baby to make it better. Your children were the temporary distraction for not having the missing piece filled. It was an old familiar way to avoid the pain and feel the old familiar feelings of abandonment that created the internal fear of *I will be abandoned.* I must be abandoned, and I deserve to be abandoned. Jack's seeking sex outside of the marriage has become a painful wedge and both of you are in pain. It is important Wendy that you come to understand that this is more about sex as a distraction and need to fill the void of his missing piece than it is about betrayal and loss of love. The affair is also a way that both of you avoid and deny feelings altogether. Therefore, with no emotions involved, you can go a long time without feeling the pain that you both are functioning alone and separately together.

When the feelings do rear their ugly head you can understand how overwhelming it would be. In both families it is unpredictable what will happen if one expresses their feelings. In the obvious family, if the addict is drunk or drug affected and someone expresses a feeling, they might become physical or rage. In the looking good family, they don't express them out of fear of survival and the abandonment that would happen either verbally or nonverbally. Either way, you are out! It is just as bad. If you express feelings you would be cast out and suffer extreme rejection. Whereas in your family, Wendy, acting out would be the perfect way to   go. How incomprehensible it is to imagine never being able to express your feelings to anyone in order to keep the family secrets. And if you do, you truly are abandoned by family members. They withdraw verbally and emotionally.

What you have in this family relationship is a stigma against losing control of yourself. The stigmas is that it is bad, not cool, not acceptable, and most of all shameful. Something is wrong with me. Again it's about appearances. How would it look to everyone? So you don't ever let on that you are mad. You would never let that happen...you don't cry at funerals. You don't act inappropriately. That means you go back to the rule book that tells you which way to act and that's what you do. What happens to all the feelings again? They are turned inward, which promotes stress related illnesses versus externally related illnesses. There is no conscious awareness of the feelings. Most of us know the physical sensations that occur with feelings like butterflies in the stomach, breathing changes. When someone like Jack, coming from the looking good family comes into treatment and begins to experience feelings, the therapist often will have to tell Jack to breathe. They are so detached from their feelings; they are unaware of their physical response so they stop breathing (As a   therapist it is painful to see someone that has abandoned themselves both emotionally and physically.)

Since they are so shut off they will also have a physical reaction before they are even aware of the pain, such as a headache, stomach or digestive problems, or back pain. In this family, because feelings are not allowed, they will often medicate. So this type of family system will often seek out distractions. Dysfunctional families might seek over the counter meds, alcohol, drugs, sex, or porn. They might only see a doctor for physical results of their addiction or physical cuts, bruises, broken bones, sexually transmitted diseases - either as a result of conflict with the addict when they are in a mood altered state, or because they are preoccupied with the other person's needs in their life and how they are going to meet them, they have accidents.

Wendy begins to cry once again.

Wendy: I run into doors often, never seeing them. I arrive at my destination without knowing how or what route I took to get there.

Dianne: The difference with Jack's looking good family is that no one in Jack's family will usually go into public using chemicals or sexually acting out like your father would. Jack's family would drink at home, look at porn and masturbate in the privacy of the home. Even the one affair has been sneaking around in out of the way places or becoming involved in the activities when everyone is asleep. If Jack's family had any of the other addictions and compulsions such as food, it would be acceptable. (But don't get fat.) If someone did, this would no longer be acceptable and would be punished through shaming. Thus, this would lead to binging. Or maybe things would be acted out in extremes such as exercise, extremely obsessed on healthy eating and special diets. Another compulsion could be shopping. After all, the preacher, his wife, and children must dress the part and be fashion models for the communities. After all Jack's, family is all about appearances. So one must look and be good. Have they ever been obsessed about the house and the yard and it being perfect, Jack? Was your mother obsessed with cleaning and neatness? Does she criticize you and how you keep your house, yard, or how you dress?

Wendy: I often become angry with my mother-in-law and my husband for this very reason. Most of all, it really makes me angry when he won't defend me against his parents.

Dianne pauses and waits. Since no one talks, she continues.

Dianne: Often in families like your husbands, if any drug use is a problem, the family member would most likely use prescribed medications that can be rationalized and explained as necessary after all they are prescribed by a doctor and needed for a health problem.

Wendy: I do recall that Jack often mentioned that he did not like the effects of the meds the doctor prescribed for his mother since it caused her to sleep all day. When I asked Jack why his mother needed the meds he said she got nervous over his dad's pressure on her to be perfect. He said that it had become a joke between him and his dad's conversations. He would ask, "Did Mom take her meds today?" His dad would respond, "Of course she did. After all it rained today, it didn't rain today, I spoke to her harshly today, I didn't speak to her today, the dog barked today, the dog didn't bark today. Whatever, you know she always needs a nerve pill to get through the day on the couch."

Dianne continues to explain to both of them.

Dianne: Because your mother is using medications to avoid her feelings, it would never occur to you Jack that addictions existed or that they had any effect on you or your family. What it did is cause you to internalize your feelings and fears, and it was not safe for you to reach out to anyone because of your family's status in the community. The survival skills you learned were *don't talk, don't feel,* and most of all, look good while you are "manning up." So if anyone died, they would be offered a nerve pill to allow them to show a neutral face to the rest of the world. It is never, ever acceptable to show emotions in public.

Wendy begins to cry.

Wendy: It all makes sense now. I understand why, when I want to talk or bring something up, he doesn't want to talk. He withdraws and isolates, not talking to me at all. He always becomes the perfectionist and becomes super critical and judgmental of me and the kids.

Dianne: Let me guess, so a lot of your discussions would be about how others should live and how bad others are for not being that way. Another thing Wendy, can you imagine how difficult and painful that would have been for Jack to have grown up with the constant critical atmosphere, because it back fires sooner or later. You become the object of criticism, if you are in his family. The things both of your families have in common are the comfort with crisis.

In Jack's looking good family they will handle crisis by becoming frantic in their activity being constantly busy with social events, car pools, committees, doctor's appointments, and work. They are constantly involved with other people who are needy. Another thing that your families share in common is isolation. Let me ask you, how often do you or Jack, when fighting, separate and isolate? Your family and Jack's family are also very lonely people, who don't have any other human being they can share with or depend on. They wouldn't let on, of course (self-abandonment). Nor would they know how to share, if they had someone. They do not know how to ask for their needs to be met.

Jack's family doesn't look any better than yours. Am I right?

Wendy: No. Both of our families were messed up. Now I can see how we conflict and why. It is painful, and I don't want my kids to repeat this pattern. It is too painful.

Dianne: It was probably at this point that Jack's parents decided it was time for a distraction. I bet this is where Jack came into being-a life time and a nine-month distraction was conceived.

So Wendy, go back to where the visual of Jack's parents standing back to back, with fingers pointing over their shoulder at each other and the other arm at their side with their fists clenched. Now insert your husband Jack standing with his back to his parents, his hands in his pockets. (He was never allowed to get too close or touch anyone.) Now both parents move the arms that are pointing over their shoulders and rest their elbows on their son's shoulders, pointing their finger at each other. (What a relief! Someone to come between them, supports, and bear the weight of their relationship when Jack was born.)

See how similar the pictures of both your families are alike? Both your parents are angry at each other, even though they express the anger in different ways. Part of the anger is that they have to depend on each other to keep the missing piece or abandonment wounds at bay. No one can move without affecting the other.

So Wendy, now you are beginning to understand Jack's parents, how they met and married, along with how John's family could have looked good to others, but in many ways are similar to your family, in their messages to both you and Jack. Has Jack told you anything about what it was like for him? Tell me about that.

Wendy: Well, Jack was "lucky" he was an only child. He didn't have a brother to take care of like I did.

Dianne: Can you also see how that might have been difficult in other ways?

Wendy: Well yes, he has said there was a lot of pressure. He even says sometimes he thinks it was worse for him than me, and that sometimes he thinks I am exaggerating how bad it was. He says that I should just accept what happened to me, "suck it up," move on, and stop making a big deal out of things and accept him for who he is, and that after all I picked him. When he says that, it just sends me over the edge, and we always end up fighting. Sometimes I think he does it on purpose just to piss me off and start a fight, because he shuts down and stops talking. Often he will leave or turn on the T.V., ignoring me. I go to the bed room, take a hot bath and cry or just go to bed and cry. (Something like Jack's mother did, with her nerve pills.) It's embarrassing because the children ask, what is wrong with Mom? John tells them that I'm just being my usual hysterical self, that I'll be fine. Then we act like nothing ever happened and go back to normal. I'm sick and tired of that. I want to have a better relationship. Jack is the man I love, but I can't live the rest of my life like this. It is getting worse and worse. It is affecting the kids and I don't want them to have to go through what I went through growing up.

Dianne: I understand this is painful for you, but let's go back for a minute to what it was like for Jack in his family. Jack stated one time that it really upset him because he had to always be the go-between for his parents. He said they would talk to each other through him, making him feel trapped, and in a no-win situation.

Wendy: Like with me? He even said I used the kids when he just wants to be left alone, especially when I'm in "one of my moods". Jack says that when I tell the kids, "Just ask your father," it makes him angry and makes him want to ignore me more. He says he can relate to how it makes our kids feel, because it brings back when his Mom and Dad put *him* in the middle.

Dianne: Can you see some of the beginnings of covert abuse that might have started for Jack? And the anger that can occur and how it gets acted out in your relationship?

Wendy again becomes tearful.

Wendy: I just thought he was punishing me and blaming me for our fight.

Dianne: Jack may not recognize the root of how these feelings started for him, but the feelings and reactions are on auto pilot when triggered. Because you respond the same as his parents, he deals with the situation like he did as a child, withdrawing and shutting down. The other way Jack's parents might have talked through him could have been his mom saying something like, "Well, there goes your Dad again. Work, work, work. He cares more about others than he does about us." She doesn't say anything about this to Dad himself, only to Jack. Mother goes about life as if it were a normal way of communicating.

Wendy: Yes, he has done that with our kids. I've over heard him sometimes saying to them, "Well there goes your mother again, in her mood. Leave her alone. She'll get over it." That really makes me fighting mad and instead of confronting him, I take my bath, cry, and pretend it never happened. He will often bring it up. He say to me, "Maybe you fight like you do in your family, but my family was lucky. We didn't have yelling and screaming in our family and I'm not your dad." This makes it worse, because he never defends me when his mother tells me I'm doing something wrong.

Dianne: Do you think you can now see how this is the way Jack maintained his sanity? Through his entrapment into his parents' marriage, he did no responding, just "hearing." He then acted as if nothing happened.

Wendy, tearful and angry, responds.

Wendy: I see how he sees his mom constantly criticizing me and ignores it. I'm his wife. He should defend me, and tell her to stop.

Dianne: You see, when this occurs, he responds like the child and repeats his childhood response. He is repeating the role he played in his family system.

Wendy: I see it, and that is what I would like him to work on in here. I want him to recognize his issues and work on changing them.

Dianne: What would happen if he decides not to get help, Wendy? What can you change? We can't make Jack change. We can help you make changes, and maybe that will in some way make Jack look at his responses to your new behaviors. I would like you to begin to feel the feelings on what your response will be should Jack choose not to make changes.

Wendy: This is painful. I don't know. Right now it is painful and makes me so angry, just like my parents. They will never change. I don't know how long I can live like this.

Dianne: So your tolerance for emotional pain is beginning to break.

Wendy: Yes, I guess so. Jack is so good in many ways.

Dianne: Let's go back and look at how Jack was affected in his family that has created the Jack you fell in love with.

Wendy: OK. Well he always talks about how in his family he had to be super good. When he reached adolescence he was angry at always having to be perfect and the pressure was unbearable. He became rebellious to all the rules instilled in his family. He was always under constant pressure to do and be more and more perfect in all areas of his life. Even though the messages from his family were always, "You know we love you and we know you can't always be perfect Jack." He worked harder and was always falling short. He beat himself up, until at about age seventeen when he made a decision.

After his date with his girlfriend and her pressure to be the perfect love of her life, he would do anything and everything that went against his family values. Concentration in school was impossible; his grades began to slip, because all Jack could think about was having to be a hero on the football field. So now, not only were his parents pressuring him to be perfect, but so were his class mates, coaches, and teachers.

Jack: My girlfriend, the head cheerleader from the perfect family, was pushing me to sleep with her and make a commitment. I was not even sure I wanted to go to college. I didn't know if I wanted to follow in my parent's footsteps. So at seventeen I felt things couldn't get any worse. Slowly, but surely, I began to rebel. First, my grades started slipping. My parents, being their perfect selves, said that it was a phase and that I would get through it. I quit the football team and the coach yelled and gave me grief for weeks. When I quit the team, my girlfriend quit me. I began to sneak out of school and church on Sundays to smoke. I got a part time job at the local grocery store sacking groceries. I saved up enough money to buy a Harley. My reputation changed from that of the preacher's kid to bad boy. That was fine with me.

For the first time I felt free. At eighteen I had made a transformation that my parents did not understand, and I was always the topic of their arguments. Right after high school, with my paycheck in hand, clothes in my backpack, I hopped on my Harley and headed for new frontiers. I left my parents behind feeling somewhat relieved that they could return to being the upstanding members of the community, and hoping that one day I would return as the upstanding citizen they had raised. I made it about five hundred miles to a small town and I realized I needed more money to ride off again on the adventures that lay ahead for me. I rented a small room in an old hotel and got a job as a stacker at the local store. After all, that was what I was good at. After a week they decided I would do well in produce. Actually, the produce guy left and they needed someone to fill in. It was a raise, and I could move on faster the more money I made. I became friends with some of the other sackers and began to hang out at the coffee bar - the new place to be at with the *in* crowd. This is where I met Wendy. The rest is history.

I don't have any regrets, even though sometimes we fight. You are high strung and emotional, but you love me and understand me and my moods. We have great kids, I like my job, and I get to hunt, fish, and drink beer with my friends, watching games on T.V. during football season. My parents accept you even though you don't like my mom. You say she criticizes you all the time. I never hear her do that. I think, because your parents were so critical and abusive, you are too sensitive. You going to therapy is ridiculous, but if it will help you get off my back at home and stop your constant need to change our relationship, it's a small price to pay.

Wendy's fear of abandonment becomes magnified and she, at Diane's encouragement, begins to attend twelve step meetings.

Looking at herself is painful for Wendy, and looking at how she settles for crumbs in her relationship makes her struggle harder to make Jack change, hoping one day she will be worthy of the whole loaf. Jacks mother's interference becomes more and more intolerable. Cindy would tell Jack, "If Wendy loved you; she wouldn't be acting that way. I think that therapist is hurting her more that helping her. After all, she has said things to me lately. She has said that she is setting "boundaries" with others. What kind of thing is that to say to your family?"

Jack in turn is backing up his mother, and since Wendy has stopped enabling Jack, he becomes more and more angry with her.

In a following session, Wendy confesses to Dianne:

Wendy: Part of me knows that I need to change, but my fear is that if I do, he will leave me and the children.

Dianne and Wendy begin to explore her fears and feelings. Working through her grief and losses of what never was in her relationship.   Intimacy,   healthy   boundaries,   healthy communication, healthy love had never existed. Only the dream and the fantasy had. It was all an illusion made up in her mind. Reality sucks at first for Wendy, but as she begins to grieve and live in the reality of her life, she becomes stronger and holds true to her boundaries. This makes her self-esteem, self-love, self-abandonment, and abandonment wounds to begin to fall away.   Her life is still not perfect, but it is at least more manageable and giving her some peace.

Growth for Wendy will be slow, and whether or not Jack changes, leaves, or if she leaves, Wendy will be OK. And if Wendy is OK, her children will have a chance to break the cycle that had been set into place. They will begin to heal and change for the better, giving them a chance to grow up and have healthier and happier lives, producing new generations of healthier cycles and a decrease in self-abandonment and abandonment wounds. Looking back, Wendy now knows that she could not have taken her journey of recovery without the grief process and the help of others outside of her internal family system.

******

Ask yourself, are you like Wendy? Can you afford not to start your journey to your inner peace, instead of looking for your missing piece? Or are you Jack, willing to accept what life gives you, and always feel the hole that lives within you that keeps you searching for your missing piece through addictions, dysfunctional relationships, and dysfunctional families? Are you continuing the painful cycle of grief, unresolved pain, and need to fill that gaping hole that comes from avoiding your journey to reattach to God, and gain your missing peace for yourself and generations to come?

What do you think the outcome of Wendy and Jack's story will be? What do you think yours will be when you have all of the information about self-abandonment and abandonment wounds in this book? What will your outcome be? Whatever it is, I hope in some way this will break your dysfunctional cycles and bring you the peace you deserve as a perfect child of God. You owe it to yourself and the generations to come.

Recovery is a choice we make individually and it's not dependent on everyone being in recovery for one to be well and obtain their inner peace. Peace is internal and allows one to move through life in a spiritual way, accepting what life has to give and receiving with gratitude.

Now for the theory.

 The fear is that if I let go or turn my back on my core beliefs I will abandon my family and God, and if I abandon them, I'll be alone. Then the survival instinct of the child part of me kicks in and keeps me stuck in my family role that I play in the system.

It's the fear of being alone and being alone=being unloved which is often then reinforced by the dysfunctional family system that makes me continue to not give up or change my role.

We can stop blaming.

The Second Encounter- It's NO encounter

It's a painful, self-sabotaging, blaming place to be-for self and others

The cycle is breakable

Chapter 4

The Pecking Order

**The answer is through resolution of the issues of
abandonment wounds and the reconnection to God.**

Operating Out of a Role by Any Other Name Would be the Same

Throughout one's life, in all personal, professional, and other relationships, individuals tend to act and react in accordance with the childhood roles they have chosen. The key word here is 'chosen'. They assume (remember that to assume, makes an ass of you and me) and play out these roles at home, in school, on the job, in social settings, relationships of importance, and everywhere else they go. Later in life, many also impose these roles onto their own children, thus perpetuating a cycle that can often have very harmful, long-term effects. You see, each role can either be played in a constructive or destructive way, depending on the degree of the family's dysfunction and the severity of problems stemming from the core issue of abandonment wounds. However, these are simply choices that individuals make. Remember that change, too, is a choice. At any time in one's life, a person can decide to change his or her roles. They can also alter the destructive way he or she acts out their existing role, and begin playing it in a healthy, constructive way.

An individual can even choose to stop playing roles all altogether. In order to do this however, he or she must first realize they have a problem with the current role they are playing. He or she needs to understand how and why they made these choices about their roles. The individual must then come to understand the reasons why he or she developed such a strong attachment to his or her role. Remember, no one does anything without getting something out of it, whether it is a positive or negative reward. Remember, you will evaluate which reward you feel the most comfortable receiving. Finally, the individual must learn how to break the cycle of pain and grieve his or her losses. Those losses they have had as a result of staying stuck in the self-destructive part of their role. For it is only turning within, that one can never go without. Think about that one for a minute and ask yourself: how can I turn within for the answers?

The answer is through resolution of the issues of abandonment wounds and the reconnection to God.

What's with a Pecking Order?

First, we must look at what is a system. Remember that in the beginning I said I wanted you to get to know and think of everything as a system.   Well this is the reason, so listen up.

Everything is based on a system, and the family is no exception. Think of the family as a mobile and that all the pieces must be in its place, otherwise the mobile will become off balance and will flounder until it can adjust to a new center of balance. However, even if the piece of the mobile is placed back on the mobile, it will flounder once again, until it returns back to its original balance. What's the point?   Once the part of the mobile is removed for the first time, there is no going back without a period of time of being off balance. Since the family system likes to maintain homeostasis (or balance, if you will) at all times, each member of the family must pick their role and maintain that role to keep the family in balance.

When one of the family members decides to disconnect or change their role, so to speak, the family will resist the change and for a period will attempt to get the changed member to return to their original role. This is now not just about maintaining homeostasis, it is now also about staying in the family comfort zone and can often be a stressor that can determine if the family will survive or not.

After the mobile has reached a new level of balance, or homeostasis, that new balance is the beginning of a new norm for that system.

The family comfort zones are about developing family norms. A norm is what is predictable with each family member and their response to each other. This is based on how each member reacts to each other in a predictable manner, so that no one has to change and step out of their behavioral or an emotional zone with each other.

How many of you have experienced, for example, something similar to the following scenario. In my family, my sister and I used to keep things from our Dad, because we knew that his response would be one of anger and rage if it was something we knew he wouldn't want to hear. However, if we told Mom first, she would only break it to Dad if it was necessary, thus keeping the family system status quo. Think of examples that have occurred in your family system that have caused ripples or maybe even an earthquake in your life and journal (that's right; in detail). If you like, ask a family member that was involved in the same incidents to do the same, and I'll bet you both have a completely different take on the incident. Ever wonder why that happens? Well it is because you are operating from different roles within the family system. I am getting the horse before the cart a little here, which I have been known to do.

I hope I have tantalized you enough to read on so you can decide which role you played in your family system, to understand the significance and importance of these five roles, to look at how you chose your role, to identify how you continue to play your role throughout your life, and to know how you self-sabotage (if you continue to play the role as you have been). Let's face it, you would not have picked up this book if somewhere you did not want to change self– destructive behaviors that have not gotten you what you want out of life. Therefore, I will back up for a moment and talk about pecking order. There are many books and articles written on this subject that are very interesting, so I will leave research up to you. I will only focus here on what pertains to abandonment wounds, self-abandonment, and self-sabotage which cause one to look outside of one self for one's missing piece.

What's order got to do with it?

Birth order system

According to birth order people that follow this sort of thing, how individuals turn out depends on the order in the family chain they were born in. Science is beginning to prove that this theory has validity. In the five roles of a family, I will use order as a base and become more in depth of exactly how it can affect one's life, giving the positive and negative sides of the roles. So with this in mind, let's get started with an order overview.

If you are the first born child, your profile might look like this. You may be better educated than your younger siblings. You are more concerned with meeting your parent's expectations and needs. You are more likely to serve as the family historian and the guardian of elderly parents when the time comes. You have a higher I.Q. than your younger siblings do (so if you are so smart, why didn't you give all the responsibilities to your younger siblings? Oh that's right, you are the responsible one. Sorry I asked). You are likelier to hold a professional position. (Finally, something to brag about.)

If you happen to be the middle child, you may take longer to choose a career than your other siblings. You may feel and actually be less connected to family, and more connected with friends outside of the family system. You may de-identify from your first born sibling, making opposite life choices, which to the family system can be seen as a defiant behavior at the time. You might have experienced the lack of parental recognition your first born sibling enjoys. You will almost always develop self-esteem issues.

If you are the youngest born in a family system, you are more tolerant of taking risks than your siblings. You are often physically smaller than your first born sibling. Your are more likely to be artistic, an adventurer at heart, and a self-motivated entrepreneur. You are less likely to be vindicated than your first born sibling. Last but not least, you are frequently funnier than any of your other siblings. (If you only saw partial glimpses of yourself, do not fear; you have not been left out of the equation. Read on, you are in here).

Popping out of the womb in the right order

Or

What's a Role got to do with it?

In order to survive in a family system (there's that word again), every child learns to play one or more roles according to the number of siblings in the household. Each sibling will adopt and practice their role(s) and continue to play them long after they grow up, leave home, and establish independent lives of their own. However, before I define those roles and illustrate how they apply to virtually everyone, let me interject a question. By now, you are probably starting to see how the core issue of abandonment wounds could even begin before we are born and how it affects us so often throughout our lives. With that in mind, are you also beginning to identify how this core issue has had a dynamic effect on your own life?

Regardless of your answer, fear not, because EVERYONE has issues that relate back to abandonment wounds. So now, let us take this a step further. It is the severity of the abandonment an individual experienced in the beginning that determines how one will play the role(s) one adopts for oneself as children and keep playing all our lives. This is done as a form of protection against others, and it allows an individual to stay in dysfunctional relationships or self-sabotaging behaviors. Most of all, however, playing these roles provides a person with the ability to maintain denial of one's self, so that they can remain in the comfort zone of their life.

In other words, it allows us to avoid taking responsibility for where we are at in our lives and what we have attracted to ourselves. This basically serves as a rationale for remaining the same, even when change would be a positive, healthy thing. We avoid taking responsibility for where we are at in our lives because taking responsibility would lead to change, and our fear of change goes back to our core fear of consequences (what if ...). More specifically, this form of denial and avoidance helps stave our innate fear of being abandoned off (the fear of being left alone), and most of all, our fear of being unloved. Now comes the core issue (again) of loss of identity, loss of spirituality, and the loss of unconditional love-which equals abandonment wounds. With all that said, let us begin to look at how this is acted out in our lives. My theory of abandonment wounds and self-abandonment centers on the development of five different roles we play in order to remain somewhat stable and dependable, even when all the people and the chaos in our lives seems out of control or unbearable.

When we discover that the tones our parents use are meant to convey their moods and pleasure or displeasure, we soon learn something that is complicated, yet simple at the same time. We learn that if we do what pleases Mom and Dad, they will love and not abandon or withdraw from us. So we become attuned to their moods and needs and ignore our own. We become an adult before we know how to handle it physically or emotionally, thus overcompensating and becoming Mom and Dad's caretakers versus them being ours. In doing so, we learn that unless we can act as the grown up or adult and be perfect, we cannot be assured of the security we get from our family's love or know that our family won't abandon us.

Since we are still unable to take full care of ourselves, we need to keep our parents happy for survival - even though we now believe they may be happy only because we are performing as they want us to. We may also still be lacking something within ourselves. Therefore, we can come to believe we are flawed and can never be good enough no matter what we do. This in turn creates the need to be a human *doing* versus a human being.

Thus, we *think I am not OK unless I can perform to perfection 24/7.* Since we are not OK with others or ourselves, and since no one can do all things and be all things to others all the time, we will always reinforce the fact that we somehow come up short.

How abandonment and roles are linked

In the theory of abandonment there are five roles, briefly mentioned previously, that are played in order to maintain balance within the family system. I would like to cover each of those roles now in detail. There are good and bad sides to every role and each one of us can choose which good or bad side to play, based on our belief from our past files. We choose which side we should play to accomplish our goal in each given situation. For example, if in the past when something good has happened to me as a result of using one of my positive behaviors from my given or chosen role in the system and I get the results that I like, I will store those thoughts somewhere in the files of my brain and pull them out for reuse when similar things happen in the future and I want good results. The same is true for the negative things that happen in my life. I will go through the files in my brain till I find one that worked in the past and replay it. The problem is that they don't always work. So bringing the past into the future will only create the past, which never works in the future, as they are two separate things.

Remember that all humans are neither good nor bad. We are simply individuals who do good and bad things and as a result, create good and bad things in our lives. Furthermore, we can only recreate what we have learned and most often, what we learned has not completely been the truth.

With that said, let us look at the roles of the pecking order in families. These roles can change order when one person chooses to pass on their role to another sibling or simply gets tired of playing that role. A person can make a conscious choice to change the role and work towards recovery of recreating his or her past over and over again.

The first role is most often, but not always, the first born within the family system, and is often referred to as the Hero or sometimes the Super Hero or Adult Child.

Role #1: Hero, Super Hero, Adult Child

This role is often the first born in a family. As the parents have never had children before, most often they are treated more as young adults. Consequently, they behave more mature at a younger age. They operate internally from the feelings of inadequacy, guilt, and hurt. The negative side of this role functions and uses the following as their defense mechanism when responding to others or life situations: denial. This role goes into denial that they cannot gain or get control of the situation or problem. Since they operate out of the need for approval from others, they must deny anything less than perfection. They appear to others as the one that has it "all together." They are what I call super achievers and will never quit until the job is done right. They are highly driven and often have stress related diseases as a result of the pressure they put on themselves, such as ulcers, high blood pressure, etc. They can often feel unemotional, aloof, detached, uncaring, and in control while quite the contrary is true. It is the defenses they use to not show the pain and fear of not being accepted and admired by others.

In other words, Heroes are so busy being the external heroes to others; they are unaware of their internal feelings. Others see them as successful in everything they do. They often make others feel inadequate or as if they can't live up to their example. Heroes are super responsible and will walk into any situation and immediately take control, organizing and delegating and redoing projects that others have done as they are never satisfied and often feel it would be easier to just do it themselves. They often feel that they are special and deserve privileges that others don't get, since they work harder than others in order to gain approval and recognition. There is something to be said for the Hero. If you want something done just tell the Hero and they will get it done. They are also caretakers of the other roles. They feel as if it is their duty to parent their siblings and when grown, they repeat the pattern at work.

This also creates an internal anger that can come out as criticism, sarcastic remarks, or put downs when they feel overwhelmed and feel super responsible for everyone else. They work really well with the Jester or Mascot role, as that role has a hard time being taken seriously. Heroes can take the mascot's creative ideas and put them into action. This often creates friction as the Hero gets the credit, promotion, and raise for the other roles' ideas or problem solving solutions. They have a hard time seeing why others would be resentful of them since they feel, after all, they got it done or fixed it. As a Hero they often become overwhelmed and exhausted in this drive to gain their self-worth.

Role #2: Rule-breaker, Defiant, Problem Child

Usually, but not always, this role is the second born within the family system. They often are the one in the family that takes on the role of distractor and is often influenced by peers more than any other role. Since they often feel disconnected from the family, both emotionally and physically, they seek a sense of belonging from their friends or their families, often wishing that they were a member of their friend's family rather than their own. They tend to idealize their friends' parents and are unable to see that their friends' families have problems as well. Usually, they will choose like-minded peers that are rebellious or walk the thin line of moral and legal rules. They often find themselves defiant and resentful of others in authority as they take out and act out the frustrations and denial of the dysfunction in their own family, projecting the anger towards others that they perceive has having authority over them.

Often this is the child that will grow up to develop addictions and act them out. They are attention-seeking and are viewed by others as the one that always needs to be in the lime light or take control. Either way, they must have the focus as they believe through their sacrifice they are protecting the ones they love. Most people playing the Rule-breaker role become love addicts and get involved with love avoidants, setting themselves up to be hurt in no-win situations or relationships. They have the need to fulfill the need they have to be loved, yet they feel unworthy or unlovable, and must suffer. The Rule-breaker role also has difficulty with success and job achievement and recognition. They are often labeled the *wild card* or the *trouble maker.* They are resistant to change and often seen as a non-team players. They usually become sullen when met with confrontation or rejection. They will hold onto grudges and have difficulty with forgiveness, without first attempting a plot for revenge on those they perceive as having hurt them. They will always act out versus acting in. They keep others connected to them through withdrawal creating the love addict-love avoidant in relation to others in their lives. Intimacy is often an issue as they feel it is not safe to let anyone know they have been hurt. So in order to avoid that from happening, they keep others at a distance having no close relationship with anyone; even themselves. Internally, they operate from hurt, using anger as a way to cover up fears and rejection. These personalities will always provide focus and distraction for others in their family, friend, or coworkers. They have a tremendous need to take the punches to protecting others, which makes them extremely susceptible to severe codependency and other addictions that create stress-related diseases and early deaths.

Codependency is the new buzz word for what ails you and appears in almost all the roles, but more so in this Risk-taker role.

Because it is important to see where and how this terminology *codependent* fits in with the abandonment theory and all the new surge of process addictions such as sex, love avoidant, eating, shopping, and any other addictive behaviors that occur in ones life, we now fit these into the new category known as process addictions. These are new terms used in the counseling field to explain and put labels on what I have come to believe is nothing more than the byproduct that occurs in one's life when one becomes spiritually bankrupt.

There are massive amounts of self-help books available on these above listed topics, and I want to remain focused on the issue of abandonment. Each topic deserves volumes within themselves. So if you are interested in these other addictions, just shop the self-help recovery section of your book store or just go on-line and type in the topic, and you will be inundated with literature on these subjects. The bottom line is, the greatest killer in the country today is stress related diseases that are for the most part induced by the emotional spiritual bankruptcy that is occurring in the world today.

I would like to introduce you to a new terminology that I think will become significant within the next few years and explain why this terminology is so important to the reconnection to one's self and the breaking the cycle of abandonment. The term *is bio entanglement* which simply put means the inner connection we have with each other on a soul to soul level and the total connection with all that is in our universe, through our root system called life. Each one of us is spiritually connected so when I am in distress with my detachment from God, it will have the stone on the water or the butterfly effect, if you will. It will affect everyone.

Codependency says to heal one must detach with love. I am saying it's exactly the opposite. I am saying the problem is we have not attached with love to support and share our spiritual connection with each other out of the fear that in attaching, we will lose ourselves. I have found the opposite is quite true. Attaching in love, spirit, compassion, and nonjudgment produces strength in numbers. This is why the twelve step support groups have become so abundant. It is about the attachment in the spirit of love, not in rules and strings.

No wonder co-dependency is so painful.   It is the rules and strings (or if you will, irrational, dysfunctional beliefs) that are bread out of dysfunctional family systems passed down from generation to generation that will have a ripple effect on all of humanity including all living things as Spirit exists in everything. After all, we were all created by the same God.

If you have noticed that I have not backed off of the main theme and solution.   Since the very beginning, the problem and the solution are one in the same and the treatment is bio entanglement.   Self-healing is the reconnecting that must occur to heal our self and others.   The Bible makes the statement that "we are created in His image" which if taken as a truth, simply means we are our creators.   One can choose to create from the spirit of nonjudgmental, love, and joy without expectations, which is acting out of compassion, versus the dysfunctional family beliefs that were passed down as a result of the generational curse.

Role #3: Lost Child, Hidden Child, or the Invisible Child....

The Mr. Cellophane's of the world - you can walk right by me, right walk through me, and never see me and never know I'm there

Individuals that are trapped in this role are often not ever noticed and are often over looked within the family, at work, and any other relationships.   They take on all the pain in relationships and suffer in the silence of their own mind or a safe hiding place where they can escape into day dreaming and fantasy. This is the role that was so well portrayed in the movie Home Alone, where the family did not even notice that the child was missing till they were on the plane. This role has trouble with finding their own voice or identifying their own feelings. They have been so use to feeling for others that they are often not even aware that they have any feelings of their own. The Lost Child feels like they are they emotion-keeper, while the Hero is the behavior-keeper in the system. The Lost Child, as grownups, often continues to live in fantasy, not seeing relationships as they really are. They develop fantasies around their relationships to avoid seeing the dysfunction and facing the painful reality. When the denial can no longer by denied, they more often than any other role, become so depressed that suicide might often become the only option they see as an escape from the pain.

They are extremely sensitive and often have difficulty with someone expressing themselves honestly or setting limits. They see it as a personal rejection and they become overwhelmed with extreme fears of abandonment. These individuals have a hard time with faith and believing in God. They truly feel alone and are often the one that feels the most need to belong. The hunger and emotional starvation they feel make them a great candidate to become involved in relationship addictions as well as other addictions. They also mistake sex as love and will become promiscuous just to feel loved, but since they see themselves as inadequate, they will beat themselves up and tell themselves they do not deserve to be loved. They set up the parodox of love-hate relatioships or set themselves up by getting involved in dead end relationships that will end up proving that, even though they are willing to give their all, it is never good enough. These personalities often create stress related diseases, suffer from or develop clinical or major depression that has a hard time responding to medications. They have an internal belief that they do not deserve to exist and will die early, often by self-inflicted ways such as accidents or suicide.

At work they often are creative and a great knack for new and inventive ways to solve problems. They are creative in the development of new ideas. Since they don't speak up, the Hero often takes their ideas, puts them into action, and takes credit for the Lost Child's accomplishments. This creates the internal resentment that causes stress related issues such as ulcers, heart, and blood pressure problems for the Lost child, or Hidden Child.

Internally, the Lost Child has an unbelievable buildup of rage and when pushed to the snapping point can end up in random acts of violence. This confuses others, causing them to state things like, "He or she was a quiet and a good person. I never would have thought he or she could have killed or hurt all these people." They live their lives out of extreme fear, confusion, and hurt. The Hidden Child will withdraw to lick their wounds and are, as a result, often seen and mistaken as being aloof. They are the most susceptible out of all the roles to having disordered eating, as they are trying to gain some type of control in their lives. They always feel that they are never in control. They feel governed by their emotions, so eating is the only self-soothing that will not abandon them. Others often see this individual as quiet and distant. They can also be mistaken as being super self-efficient and independent, when in fact the opposite is true. They are super dependent on others since the only way they can feel is if they are feeling the pain of the world. They feel they were brought here to suffer and suffer they must. Most of these people stuck in this role remain victims, feeling as if they cannot be loved or belong. This role provides the relief for the family as they relieve others of the need to feel the pain that comes with family dysfunction, relationships, or work dysfunctions. The biggest fear and most pain for this role is the fear of abandonment or rejection.

Role #4: The Jester Role or Mascot Role

The Tears of the Clown

This role is, but not always, the youngest member of the family. They provide the distraction for the family system. They are often time, the one in the system that is told they are ADD or ADHD. They are always full of energy and usually are smart, coming up with a quick wit, making light of events going on in the family to provide pain and stress relief. They are the attention-seekers. They are pulling pranks, taking the focus away from the issue at hand. Thus, he or she is the one that will also be blamed when the scapegoat needs rescuing. They deal with all emotions with humor, but inside they are fragile and usually operating out of fear, insecurity, and confusion. They are often so anxious that they have a hard time focusing and have lack of concentration. Consequently, they are often ignored and viewed as if they have few things worthwhile to share. The Hero will often come to the rescue and often implement the idea; plus often take credit for the idea themselves, creating a love-hate relationship between the Hero and the Jester Role.

Role #5: The Catch-All Role or When There is No Role Left for You

In this role, when there are more than four siblings or if you are an only child in a family, this role is exactly as it sounds. It is the role that gets stuck, if you will, and will have to play parts of all the roles so that the family system can maintain homeostasis. Whatever is not being played out at any given time, the Catch-All will have to step in and take on the opposition part of that role. This often leads this individual into confusion over *who am I* and his or her emotions are based on others' behaviors versus their own. If they even have the ability to know if they have their own feelings, this person usually is the most difficult to treat and will require a longer grieving process as they really have no sense of who they are. The Catch-All role always feels as if they are on a roller coaster with their behaviors and emotions. These are likely to seek out love or sex addictions, as they need to have constant individuals in their lives so they will know how to behave and feel. These individuals will have problems with being alone and want things that are tangible, rather than spiritual, making it difficult for them to connect spiritually. They even may become hoarders and base their entire life successes and failures on their ability to possess things. They are likely to have difficulty in relationships, because they feel being loved by more people is better. Thus, they have difficulty with affairs or difficulty with being able to commit to only one person. This playing out of the role allows them to also be many people at the same time, helping them to avoid the pain of not knowing who they really are, anyway.

All of these roles are susceptible to repeating the cycle and passing it on for generations to come. Even with counseling the energy is difficult to break. All of the roles operate out of additional feelings of guilt, shame, anger, and fear. Sometimes it is externalized and comes out in behaviors of self-pity, compulsion, aggressiveness, grandiosity, rigidity, charm, anger, seriousness, humor, powerlessness, perfectionism, super responsibility, self-blaming, and extreme manipulation. No wonder it is difficult for individuals to connect with God.

With all of this chaos going on and the need for a cortisol fix, one has a hard time to sit with quiet, non-emotion, and non-behavior space to connect with something greater than one self. This plays into the difficulty of overcoming the fear of abandonment. Based on most of our past family dysfunctions, we continue what we are so well taught: *it is not OK to be yourself even if you could figure out who that is* and the ingrained, well trained self-abandonment.

By becoming able to identify when and what triggers these emotions and behaviors, it puts the ball back in your court to either self-abandon or not. Remember, awareness plus taking responsibility equals personal power to face your abandonment wounds and reconnect with God. Life changes **can** begin to occur. Time delays on a newer, healthier life style and is slowed by the human factor. After all, with faith and belief, God manifests instantly. You are the delay. So the faster you grieve the past and fears of the future, the sooner your role can change and your new life can begin. Because it is human nature to return to the familiar, it will be a constant, daily, and even sometimes a minute by minute self–inventory to avoid relapse into old patterns and self-abandonment.

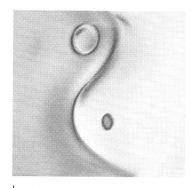

The search outside myself begins and I look to others for unconditional love, thus seeking the impossible and with this action, I have again repeated the cycle of self-abandonment to avoid the reality that I was never loved unconditionally by anyone because I did not love myself unconditionally, because I was detached from God.

God doesn't abandon you, you abandon God. When you abandon God, you abandon yourself. Thus, self-abandonment begins.

The encounter of a Third Kind:

It's about the brain wave cycles, to stop the self-sabotaging and reconnect:

(THE BRAIN, BODY, SPIRITUAL CONNECTION)

Chapter 5

In a Flash, the Theory of Self Abandonment Crystallizes

I felt it even before I knew the word or what the word meant. I don't know why it took me so long to figure it out. Maybe I missed some messages growing up, but come what may, I finally got there. One day, while teaching a classroom full of students, I had a big AHA moment. Why is it that the most life-changing, insightful moments happen in public? Could be another core belief that says that your most eye opening, emotionally shattering, and embarrassing moments must happen in public so that your skill of "sucking it up" doesn't get stale.

In front of the class, I was talking about why clients come to see a counselor. Clients don't just wake up one morning and say to themselves, "I think I need to go to a counselor." Out of my mouth came the word crisis.

I had always thought no one would just choose to begin counseling without something in their lives having spurred them into action. It is human nature for humans to need something like pain to motivate one to make a change in their lives, such as problems with their relationships, the law, work - just to only name a few. Most individuals will go through a tug of war before deciding to seek help. This battle comes up out of fear and letting go of ones' ego and super ego. In other words, it require coming to the point of acceptance and surrender that I need help - in spite of the fact that I feel guilt and shame. It requires a moment in which we realize that somehow I am inadequate to deal with this alone and must look outside. Unconsciously, I know that my system is no longer functional, because the behaviors that I used to do no longer work to numb the pain. In other words, I will have to break the dysfunctional system's *No Talk* rule.

The fear is that if I let go and ask for help, I will have to turn my back on or challenge some core dysfunctional beliefs. In doing so, I will abandon my family (breaking the most dysfunctional families' fast and hard rule: *don't talk; don't feel*). Furthermore, if I abandon my family, I will be alone. Then the survival instincts of the childhood part of the "self-kicks" in which keeps one stuck in the problem rather than moving into the solution.

A crisis has a potential to spring you to seek help.

Now back to the reason someone seeks help during a "crisis". One thing we know is that often times a person can see a crisis coming, but in spite of seeing and knowing, they are unable to stop it from happening.

Only by going back and challenging our core beliefs can we change our feelings and responses to the world around us today.

Crisis = change

Another insight about a crisis is that it always resolves itself—even if the person does nothing. Therefore, a crisis is usually short lived. When a crisis is over, most people will leave therapy. Some may not if they are suffering from obsessive-compulsive thoughts, have a low-grade addiction to chaos and trauma, or if it's mandated by a family member, a boss, or the law.

A crisis always resolves itself-even if you do nothing.

The Crisis is Over and Abandonment Begins

After a crisis, fear, change, and the issue of abandonment rears its ugly head.

Returning to the class I was speaking to, I was talking about why clients come to see a counselor. As I shared, I discover the word crisis and I follow it with the scenario of change, fear, and abandonment. So as I was writing these words on the board (you see, I had always thought that if you didn't write it down it would never happen). In the middle of writing the big A word, I inadvertently broke it apart. (I was never good at talking and writing at the same time. It's kind of like chewing gum and walking. It takes coordination.)

I shared with the students, "When clients come to counseling they see it as a form of suicide by breaking the family's "*No Talk* rule."

As I said this, I looked at the board and I had separated out the big A word so it looked like this:

A / BAND / ON / ME

Bricks fell again, light like in the delivery room, and I realized, "suicide my ass".   Clients were coming to counseling for unresolved issues of ABANDONMENT. Suicide in the family was just a consequence of 'a band on me' that went all the way back to the beginning.

Here is the cycle: abandonment, crisis, change, fear, and the loss of one's identity; so then we abandon ourselves and the cycle continues. Our core belief tells us that I'm not OK

Let's take the cut up word of a-**band**-on-me-. What is a band?

It is an unending, round circle and is often referred to as a wedding band (ringing bells, yet?) If we take the band and put an s-shaped line inside with a dot at the fat ends of the s shape, we have the yin and yang, symbols in the Orient for masculine and feminine.

A / band / on / me . . . nt   **A-band-on-me**

Now this is where it gets interesting. Go all the way back to the beginning to the original point of abandonment and all the ones we have yet to mention, and you have your loss of identity as a human being. Since in the delivery room we could not understand if our parents were happy about our sex or even our existence, later in life we assumed the worst and begin to believe, "I'm not OK as a female or as a male." This is a point in which we lose our identity, our sense of self, and our spirituality.

Since we are told that mankind was created in God's image, the image of a perfect being, it is at this point that one turns their back on their creator by coming to believe we are not perfect. We suffer a profound loss of identity or connection with the power greater than ourselves, God, or whatever you may call it in your own personal beliefs. The sense of loss, however, is very subtle and barely registers in our conscious minds.

This is when one begins to create their missing piece, which is our conscious contact with God, that allows us to be whole and perfect just the way we are. This is also when we first begin to engage in self-abandonment and denial of one's connection to being perfect in God's eyes. Therefore, one begins to self-sabotage as a result of not feeling worthy of having all that one can be or have in their lives. When one turns a blind eye to what is, it no longer exists in your world. Therefore, one begins to feel the loss without the ability to identify what it is one has lost and sets out on a journey to find one's missing piece in order to bring oneself back to one's identity and who one really is and find our missing peace.

That elusive piece is what creates your external identity through role playing in your family system and all your relationships. Your missing peace is your true identity and connectedness to God and perfection, with no need to play roles, because you are whole alone. You came alone, you go out alone, and therefore you are whole alone.

Who you are, and even if you knew, you might still feel as if you are somehow defective like a toy that has been recalled by the president of the company called Mom and Dad. Or maybe you decide you need a life partner, another person to help make you a complete human being.

One rationalizes, "Yes that will make me whole, and since I want to work on my leftover childhood issues, I'll find someone like the parent I have the most unresolved issues with. Then I cannot only make myself whole, but I can also resolve those issues with my parents while helping them heal their wounds–thus ending my feelings of abandonment. (Of course, one would take on the responsibility for another's happiness and problems, after all codependency is a breeding ground for dysfunctional systems.)

I can kill two birds with one stone, and I won't feel inadequate as I have now made my parents perfect in my eyes again, which actually makes three birds." (If nothing else, one must learn to be efficient.)

Another verbal or nonverbal message one might have received from others such as parents, siblings, friends, and teachers, could have been: *being alone equals being unloved.* Therefore, a search outside of ones' self begins to look to others for unconditional love. This sets us up for abandonment and the unachievable. By looking for unconditional love in others, one repeats the cycle of abandoning one's self in order to avoid the reality that one was never loved unconditionally by anyone, because one did not love themselves unconditionally.

So until you can forgive yourself and take responsibility of your perceptions for all that is happening, what you perceive to be both positive and negative in your life, you cannot forgive others. To not forgive is to not love unconditionally. You will always have expectations and when expectations are not met, unconditional goes out the window. For example, let's take a child whom was given negative feedback or maybe even a consequence for some failure such as forgetting a chore or bringing home a bad grade. The child's perception is 'I am not loved unconditionally; therefore, there is something wrong with me'. To add to that, maybe, his sibling brings home a good grade or a trophy for something they have done. The message becomes 'they are loved, but I still have to do something to be loved'. This then becomes part of his core belief: *I must accomplish or be perfect* (a human being not a human *doing*). This belief passes down from one generation to the next.

Regardless of whom we are, some things, like innate fear of change, are simply fundamental to being human. We all share certain basic traits and are susceptible to many of the same influences as children. Very early on we develop our core beliefs and behavioral patterns while learning from our parents and other immediate family members how to interact with others.

Shortly after birth, we also begin to adopt very distinct roles within our individual families and believe our parents are infallible or perfect. We imitate our parents–even when they make mistakes or demonstrate unhealthy behaviors. Our only point of reference to what is healthy or unhealthy is what is given to us by our parents, who may or may not know what's functional and what's not. This holds true for any role models we look up to as little children, including our biological parents, adopted parents, older siblings, or other guardians who have a dynamic impact on us during our first few years of life.

Are you beginning to see how this is all tied together? Now let us see how the left brain and right brain connect to the *A Band On Me* theory.

Chapter 6

Just When You Think You Know it All, You Know Nothing

As a therapist having studied the brain and what supposedly makes people think and do the things they do, I became even more confused and frustrated with my life and others in it. Therefore, I went back to the study of the great theorists of our time: Freud, Jung, Erickson, Gestalt, Ellis, etc. What I discovered was that each of the theories worked. They worked for the theorist, but not all clients. Therefore, I tried to integrate the theories and use what worked. The problem was, not all of them worked together and again, not on everyone. So the constant need to strategize the integration of the techniques became exhausting and took my focus off the solution to the problem, which kept me stuck in the problems, not the solution. I was stuck on the issues.

You see, I got into this field under the guise to help others (because it would be selfish to help only myself). So try as I might, no matter how many techniques out of each theory or combination I used, I was not getting results for myself or my clients. Not willing to give up on myself or others, I began to study and research again. Then the light went on. The reason it was not working for me was simple. Each great theorist came up with his or her theories born out of their own particular life circumstances, and not everybody's circumstances are the same.

So if my theory fits you, you are welcome to share it. If it doesn't, work on finding your own. Who knows, yours might help others. Warning: be aware that to find your own theory one law applies: you have to know yourself. That can be scary and painful, especially with skeletons in your closet, and there always are! One must open the door slowly so they won't all fall out at once and overwhelm oneself. With the realization that one's core issue must be made aware to the individual before one can make a decision to change; I went to work on myself (what better guinea pig). It took a great deal of soul searching and pain to go back through my family of origins dysfunctional issues, before I realized that my core issue is a universal one and shared by everyone in varying degrees. It just depends on the extent of the severity with the issue that determines how long it takes to put the core issue in remission. I say remission because most human's instinct is to return to the comfort of our original feelings and behaviors when confronted with something unfamiliar, painful, or our ego is being challenged.

People do three things at a time, according to Ellis: they think, feel, and behave. Given that scenario, one would wonder how one learns what to think about? Where do our thoughts come from, and how do you form them? Did you know that the average person thinks over sixty thousand thoughts per day? Yes, that is right, sixty thousand. And if the thoughts I think about turn out not to give me the end results I want, how can I change my thoughts to accomplish what I want?

Our thoughts are formed from our beliefs, and if any of you are like me, my family system did not instill in me very many positive beliefs; and if beliefs affect our thoughts, and our thoughts affect our feelings, and our feelings affect our behaviors, no wonder I wasn't getting what I wanted in life. So the big question is how do I change my beliefs?

How come some people can just make a decision to change their beliefs and some have problems doing so (like me). To understand the process I had to study the source, not just my family of origin dysfunction, but also how the brain processes the information it is given. In the Bible it is said that "God gave us the word and it was good." In my family and most families, the child perceives the parents' words as the word of God. Therefore, everything that was told to me by my parents was

Gospel, and I took them on as my own without question. Not all as a matter of fact, very few words were good. If we never stop to question their word, we operate from fiction. Their word may not be true. Their word was not truth. Their word was dysfunction. For example, my truth was to buy into the lies without discerning for myself. When I grew up, instead of questioning the lie, it was easier to accept it rather than challenge it. Because in challenging it, it meant I had to make a change. It's not change we fear, it's the consequences of the change we fear. Therefore, my fear was that I could not accept the new change in me. But in reality, it's about making a decision to change or simply a decision to do something different. It means I must give up control. When in truth, control is an illusion. I never really had it. Human nature always says I have to have control when in reality we aren't in control. It's only an illusion.

That's why most healing in people's lives occurs until they are mature or have a break in tolerance, which forces the maturity to occur. By reading this book and becoming aware of this information, you can raise your bottom and reach maturity sooner.

Oh what a tangled web we weave, in order to change beliefs

It occurred to me that there had to be a reason so many people like myself had problems with changing beliefs. If it was something as simple as changing the way you think to change your feelings and behavior in order to change an outcome, how come everyone just didn't do it when they didn't get the results that they wanted? In addition, how about the select ones who were able to do it and change their lives. What is it that they were able to do that the majority of others were not able to do? In other words, what is the "secret" or the magic trick that they were able to tap into to change their lives, their beliefs, feelings, and behaviors? What are the keys to unlocking one's ability to transform into wholeness vs. needing something outside of ones' self to fill the emptiness, known as the missing piece? In other words, how do we reconnect?

I began to wonder, did it have something to do with how our brain works, is developed, or is it a Freud thing: the Id, Ego, Super Ego, conscious or subconscious? After many years of research, studying clients and myself, these are my points of view and what I have come to understand. It works for me and on my clients. Look at it, study it, and see if it works for you. It can't hurt (well maybe it can, but then pain is a great motivator for change, is it not?)

What has to happen in the brain to change and re-connect?

First, I keep going back to the biggest book of all time, the Bible, in which two distinct things occurred for man. One was the gift of a brain that has levels of consciousness that allows us to tap into both the conscious and unconscious, to make choices based on the most balanced logical conclusions, thus hopefully making a decision that has our own best interest at heart. Therefore, it must be the process of not acting on both parts of the brain that gets short-circuited and causes us to make half decisions, if you will.

So we are right back at the point of abandonment and establishment of our missing piece. So again, it is our disconnect from God which helps us make choices that affect our life in self-defeating ways, along with replacing that connection and substituting a human such as Mother, Father, Siblings, Friends, Partners, Teachers, and all others that give us our core beliefs about ourselves and what we can and can't do in our lives.

With this in mind, I began my research. First came the Bible. The Bible is a wonderful resource of profound answers for humankind such as "The Original Sin." "The Sins of Our Father," is telling us that beliefs and events in one's life is generational. The Bible also states that, "We must become as child to enter the kingdom of heaven." Therefore, if one reconnects to God, one can break the generational cycle. It also states the truth will set you free. Isn't that true for everyone? When one faces one's personal truths or beliefs, one is now free to make choices. Making a choice for one's own highest good is the best and most rewarding choice anyone can make.

I also found that Freud talked about the Id as the instinct of man such as, life instincts, which are sexual instincts and biological urges such as hunger and thirst. The Id operates on the pleasure principal. The Ego is the logical, rational, realistic part of us and it evolves from the Id. The Ego acts according to reality and its function is to satisfy the Id's urges. The Ego is always conscious and acts on ones' perception of reality. The Super Ego sets moral guidelines that define and limit the flexibility of the ego. It represents the ideal rather than the real. It is the part of us that represents traditional values from parent to child. Freud also focused on the inner and outer levels of the brain as the conscious and subconscious as being the source that drives the Id, Ego, and Super Ego.

Then there was Albert Ellis' theory called the A B C Theory that holds that an activating event in one's life triggers a belief and because of that belief, one will determine our own consequences. There had to be more. If it is all that simple, why doesn't everybody apply these theories and principles and get the results they want? It was at this point it became clear to me that there was a need to combine spirituality, psychological theories, science, and studies of the functions of the brain to reach a conclusion and find a successful reason for myself and clients to be able to manifest a life of wholeness and reconnect with God.

We need to look at the brain, body, spiritual connection and their interaction in the journey to become whole, to no longer look for our missing piece, and stop our self-abandonment and self–sabotage that always sets us up to not make the choices that are best for us in life. This also has a link to the term codependency which has been touched upon throughout this book.

Conscious or Unconscious - That is the question

First, let us look at the science of how the brain works and how one can tap into constructive use vs. destructive use of the brain. First of all, science has proven that energy has no beginning and no end and is in everything. Therefore, as humans we are energy. Some believe that God is energy, and I am OK with whatever helps one identify that there is a power that is greater than ourselves and that we were created in the image of God. To deny that makes one abandon one's self, thus like the old saying *God does not abandon you, you abandon God* has merit. Did you know that science has also discovered that all living beings have a living pulsing force of life and use the source to stay alive? Humans have this source as well, with the addition of extras that allow us the free will to make our own choices on how we live and how we die.

The human brain operates on what is called brain waves and because energy has no beginning or end, it is the frequency at which energy vibrates in one's brain that allows the beliefs to be changed, so that the life outcomes one wants can be achieved. The brain wave frequency at which we operate within the brain is what allows us to make positive and negative choices for our lives.

Let us talk about the levels or brain wave cycles of the brain (I will try to make this simple as I don't want to get too technical). This is important because understanding brain waves and how to alter their levels, speed or frequency, is the key to change. There has been research that proves that successful people use their minds and brains differently than others, which confirms for me why some can just change and others have a difficult time making changes. So let us take a look at what science has discovered.

The brain vibrates and beats with electrical energy so many times a second, thus creating various levels of consciousness. As a new born we use only a small part of the brain so it beats at a very low level of electrical energy and is what scientists call the Delta or Theta levels, which are the slowest levels of electrical frequencies of the brain (around 4.5 to 8.0 per second). When you reach the ages of seven to fourteen the brain starts to increase in electrical frequency to 10.5 cycles per second which is known as the Alpha level of consciousness. After the age of fourteen the brain begins to increase in the electrical frequency and move into what is known as the Beta frequency, which is the electrical frequency that most people function at on a daily basis (anywhere from 20 to 25 cycles per second).

Left or Right, which is better?

Then we have the Left Brain, Right Brain phenomenon in which the left side of the brain is the side that logic comes from and the right brain is the creative side of the brain. The left side is often referred to as the masculine side and the right side is often referred to as the feminine side of the brain. What happens when one starts increasing in electrical frequencies and begins to spend more and more time in Beta and less and less time in Alpha? One decreases the ability to use both sides of the brain at the same time or use the left or the right side brain by choice. The left brain is where we store logic which can be helpful and important at times. However, to be able to create or make a change in one's self sabotaging beliefs and thus change outcomes in one's life, one must use the right side of the brain to create what you what to change - a positive change or a negative one.

To change negative past issues one has to take their brain wave frequencies back to the original frequencies at which the information was accepted into the brain. If this is not done, the "fix" you come up with for the problems you want to solve will only be temporary and will eventually collapse and cause you to relapse into the old, destructive behaviors that you wanted to move away from. It is stated in biblical terms in the Bible, "to enter the kingdom of heaven one must become as a child." In other words, your brain wave frequency must return to 10.5 cycles per second to have a permanent change occur in one's life. Now you ask, how does one do that? Well that is what this book will focus on: understanding self-sabotage, how to identify it, and change it.

Like I've said before, everything we create comes from the beginning and only by going back and challenging our core beliefs can we change our feelings and responses to the world around us today.

Are you beginning to see how this is all beginning to tie together? Now let us see how the Left Brain and Right Brain connect to the A Band On Me theory.

Healing requires a commitment and so you need to commit thirty-five minutes a day to your recovery through prayer and meditation.

Brain and Trauma ←→Trauma and the Brain
The chicken or the Egg

Fear is reaction to a possible outcome. If you cannot believe it or see it, you cannot fear it. So now, I am going to ask you to take a risk and read on. When this all starts to come together for you, it will change your life as you know it now. Just remember, the truth will set you free.

One might ask which side of the brain should one use the left or the right, and is one better than another? For the answer we must look at the brain itself in relation to one's identity and personality. Now, we know that the left side is related to logical thinking and is often referred to as the masculine side, while the right side of the brain is the creative side and is often related to as the feminine side of the brain. With this in mind, picture the brain itself and it fits right into a circle (there we go back to that old wedding band and A Band On Me).

So for the sake of science, let us look more closely to how one uses the split in the two sides of the brain to compartmentalize one's life and store one's beliefs to protect oneself. Let us take the left side of the brain first and label it the *personality* of one's self. According to psychologists, it is also referred to as the conscious part of one's self. The personality is developed in order to present the outside world the picture we want others to see. It is our face, if you will, to the world and more often than not, one is aware of the image one wants others to see. For example, if you want to live up to the Jones's you would be focused more on your material possessions or if you wanted to have others think you are a great person, you might focus on being a human doing, basing on your ability to do more than anyone else. Think for a minute how many personalities you have for every role you play in life. Personality is a conscious choice one makes and is strictly focused on the outer self. To sum it up, the left side of the brain is the personality you let others see. It is what you do and have. It is the method of communication with the world around you. For one to be healthy one must:

1. Be adaptive.

2. Join with the identity side of the brain.

The right side of the brain is usually associated with the feminine and unconscious thought. According to psychologists, the right brain is often referred to as the intuitive side of one's self. For my theory, I call this the identity part of one's self. The identity needs to have contact with the left brain to remain intact and maintain its identity. In other words, this is the real self, the self we don't want others to see, which if practiced on a continual basis, will disappear even from one's own sight. This is where one's talents, opinions, and being live.

There is no fear when connected to one's identity. When both sides of the brain are disconnected, it is where fear of intimacy takes shape. However, one must begin to understand that it is not the intimacy one fears, it is the consequences that will occur if one should take a risk and let someone see our identity.

The **masculine** side of the brain is the expression of personality, how we present ourselves to the word, and logic.	The **feminine**, intuitive side of the brain is what connects us to our identity and spirituality.

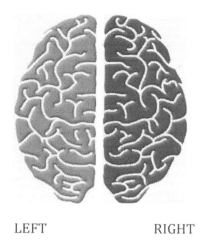

LEFT   RIGHT

ABANDONMENT AND BRAIN WAVES

BETA	*21.5*	*Age 12 - Puberty*
ALPHA	*10.5*	*Age 0 - 7*
THETA	*9.0*	*Age 1 wk – Pre birth*
DELTA	*4.0*	*Age Womb*

Pleasure and Reward –The Good, Bad, and Ugly

So now, let's talk about the area of the brain that is affected by the issue of abandonment and how that also affects one's life. I promise this will all tie together and you will be able to understand how all of this works together to help you develop a disease with yourself and disconnect from your physical, emotional, and spiritual self.

Let us talk with big words shall we? Hydrocortisone - the Cortisol factor of abuse.

Hydrocortisone is a steroid hormone, C 21 H 30 O 5, produced by the adrenal cortex that regulates carbohydrate metabolism and maintains blood pressure, also called cortisol. There is a preparation of this hormone obtained from natural sources or can be produced synthetically and used to treat inflammatory conditions and adrenal failure. Hydrocortisone or Cortisol is a steroid hormone secreted by the outer part of the adrenal gland. It is released during stress or low grade trauma reactions and has strong anti-inflammatory actions. In the synthetic form, it is injected directly into a damaged structure (i.e. an inflamed Achilles tendon) for sports injuries. The following description is what happens when cortisol is produced naturally in one's own system.

Science has been able to pinpoint the area of the brain that is affected by mood altering chemicals. It is located in the center of the brain (Amygdala) and is known as the Pleasure Center or the Reward Center of the brain. It has also been shown that the inducement of mood altering chemicals affects the production of serotonin, dopamine, and endorphins within the brain and causes the brain to shut down the brains production center. However, the brain can return to reproduction of the serotonin, dopamine, and endorphins when one stops the use of mood altering chemicals. However, in someone who has had low-grade long-term issues of abandonment, the brain will produce an over production of the Stress Hormone Cortisol. The cortisol hormone will enter the Pleasure or Reward Center of the brain and when this part of the brain has been filled, the excess cortisol hormone will over flow into the frontal lobe of the brain that affects a person's obsessive, compulsive thoughts. This causes one to be caught up in a vicious cycle of repeating negative or self-sabotaging behaviors. It is also possible that one can have the issue of abandonment occur even before one is born.

Thus, one can even be born with an addiction to low grade trauma, and when something good happens in their life, they would self-sabotage in order to recreate a familiar feeling versus a new feeling (even though the new might be good). Unlike the mood altering chemicals one might put into one's body, the hormone cortisol is a natural substance that the body produces and the production is in the control of the individual.

The low-grade addiction can and often occurs before birth, transmitted genetically or through emotional issues suffered during the mother's pregnancy. When in stress prior to birth, either low grade trauma or acute, the natural stress hormone cortisol floods her body and brain. When it does, the excess is transmitted through the umbilical cord to the fetus. Since the fetus is not equipped to handle these hormones, it causes the fetus' brain to speed up the growth of the Amygdala part of the brain which is located in the very center of the brain. It is the part that is connected to the reward center of the brain which controls appetite, stress response, and pleasure. When the baby is born, the only part of the brain that is fully developed is the Amygdala. Some say it's because of the transmission of the stress hormone cortisol that that part of the brain has to adapt and cope for survival of the fetus. When it occurs prior to birth, one can be born with a high tolerance to the stress hormone cortisol and, unless low grade or even high-grade trauma occurs to activate the excess, production of Cortisol cravings will occur and the individual will do something to activate a crisis in order to stop the cravings. These craving are much like the cravings produced with the use of other mood altering chemicals. Now you will begin to see how the theories fit together with mine of being predisposed to trauma, chaos, and stress. While it has not yet been proven that the addiction to low or high-grade trauma can become a fullblown disease like alcoholism, it certainly has the same signs and effects on the individual. Just look around you. The leading causes of death in the country today are all stress related. After all, what is more stressful than trying to fit a square peg into a round hole to feel whole?

Thus, the way to helping one's self, there must be what is called a time of reckoning and taking responsibility for one's self. One must first become aware and take responsibility to regain one's personal power.

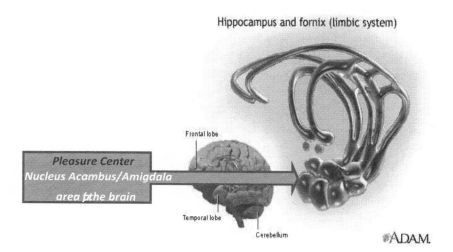

Hippocampus and fornix (limbic system)

Frontal lobe

Pleasure Center
Nucleus Acambus/Amigdala
area ƒthe brain

Temporal lobe

Cerebellum

ADAM.

Do the Chinese hold a secret?

Now let us talk about the Meridians of the body and body memories. According to Chinese medicine, just as our minds can remember all things in our life, so can the body. The meridians of the body are like a grid covering the body and flow from the spinal cord as they create the energy flow in the body to every organ and system. If the flow is obstructed, our bodies will develop poor energy flow and can lead to various mental, spiritual, or physical health problems. When the body stores memories within the body, they attach to the meridians and cause interrupted energy flow within the body. If any of you are into sports, you will recognize body memories as lactic acid. Think for a minute about being at a stop light and you look into your rear view mirror and see that the car behind you is not going to stop. You begin to tense and your muscles become tight. When that happens your body produces lactic acid. It will attach to your meridians and disturb the energy flow. This, if left untreated for a long period of time, can create major physical and emotional problems. So we also go through life collecting emotional body memories and the same response from the body will occur, because the body does not know the difference between a physically induced body memory or an emotionally induced body memory. To be able to heal body, mind, and spirit, one must also release body memories so that the energy flow can return to normal.

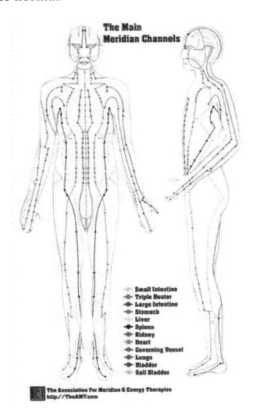

The Main Meridian Channels

Small Intestine
Triple Heater
Large Intestine
Stomach
Liver
Spleen
Kidney
Heart
Governing Vessel
Lungs
Bladder
Gall Bladder

The Association For Meridian & Energy Therapies
http://TheAMT.com

Chapter 7

Energy— I thought that belonged to the light company

My nature is to research and study to find scientific and provable information to help validate my theories. Everything I do is based on the messages I received from my family of origin that said, "What do you know about it?" and, "If someone else has an answer, then it must be so." You see if one continues to maintain black and white thinking, it is impossible to make changes because both sides of the brain are not active. So to look at science is one way to get information to validate one's new beliefs.

The other is to look at the unconventional as well. So, since I did not want to think of what is taken by some as fact, I looked for the science behind the woo-woo, which leads to the next discovery I made.

The Chakra theories is an old Chinese study like the meridians, only the chakras are located in specific positions within the spinal column in the body, and if their energy flow is interrupted it can also cause disease within the body, mind, and spirit. The chakras are not only energy spots in the body; they are related to various life circumstances and can be tuned back into healthy functioning by the use of color, light, and sound.

The first location of the core or root chakra is located at the base of the spine and resonates to the color red and the sound of middle C. It is related to the element earth and is connected to one's physical needs and feelings. It is associated with abandonment issues. According to Freud, if you want to improve the root chakra energy flow, one would have to focus on the Id.

The second chakra is located in the lower abdomen and resonates to the color orange. The sound it responds to is the sound of D. It is related to the sexuality, the identity, and emotions of the individual. According to Freud's ego theory, this would represent the Id as well.

The third chakra is located in the Solar Plexus. It resonates to the color yellow and the sound of E. It is related to fire and is connected to one's issues of power and vitality. It represents action, which would make this chakra equal to Freud's ego self. It also is related to our gut which creates our gut instinct that says, "That makes my gut hurt" when relating to gut feelings.

The fourth chakra is located and related to the heart. It resonates to the color green and the sound of F. It is the one that people associate with the feelings of love and is where one would say they hold their heart and love. It is also related to our self-motivation and self-worth through being loved.

The fifth chakra is located in the area of the throat and resonates to the color blue and the sound of G. This chakra is the one that controls one's ability to make sound and to speak one's mind. In other words, this chakra controls one's ability to make sound and is related to issues of communication and one's ability to speak up for oneself. Often people who have problems with this particular chakra will have thyroid issues and require medication.

The sixth chakra resonates to the color indigo and resonates to the sound of A. It is located in the third eye part of the body. For those that do not know where that is, it is the area right between the eyes on the forehead. It governs the element of light and controls the intuition and the ability to see.

The seventh chakra is known as the crown chakra and is located at the top of the head. It resonates to the color violet and the sound of B. It is connected to the issues of one's thoughts. It controls one's ability of understanding, and is often referred to as one's ability to know, or intuition, if you will, or one's connectedness to God.

The eighth chakra some say exists and some say it does not. Either way, it is known as the soul chakra and resonates to the color white and the sound of high C. It is located just above the head and is associated with the issues of one's sprit. This is the chakra that some say carries one's purpose in life and is the connection to one's spiritual connection to God, energy, a power greater than the self, or whatever you believe and gives an individual the will to live.

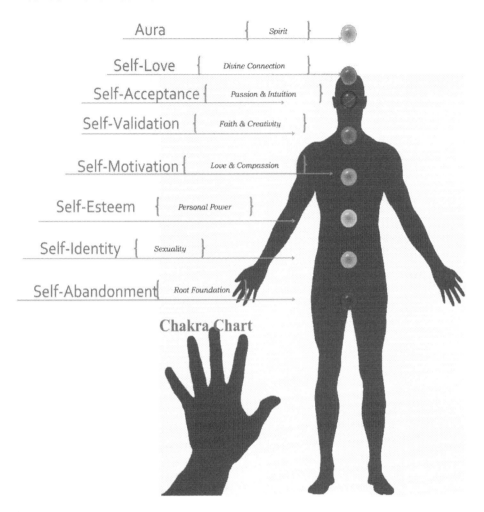

Aura { Spirit }

Self-Love { Divine Connection }

Self-Acceptance { Passion & Intuition }

Self-Validation { Faith & Creativity }

Self-Motivation { Love & Compassion }

Self-Esteem { Personal Power }

Self-Identity { Sexuality }

Self-Abandonment { Root Foundation }

Chakra Chart

The Spine: Root of all Evil or The Light at the Top?

The vertebra of the spine is what holds one together. It is the source of all nourishment to the body and is connected and supplies every organ and every system in the body and causes it to keep the body in working order. Imagine if you will, that for some reason this flow is interrupted or just gets a small flow through the system.   Think how out of whack one would become, not just physically, but also the mind and the very spirit of the individual would be out of balance. As in all systems, our nature is to be in perfect balance, and when something comes along to disrupt the balance, the system pulls together to make up for the imbalance, so that the system can be restored to (a big word) homeostasis (long word for back to normal, whether that be functional or dysfunctional-it doesn't matter). It is all about returning to the original state (more about this later).

For now, I want to focus on the chakras and the art of self-abandonment. Looking at the location and function of the chakras, I began to derive a conclusion and this is what I came up with. If the chakras are located on the vertebrae of the spine, and the spine supplies the entire body with energy flow and transmits messages from the brain to the body, and the spine is also connected to all the organs in the body and supplies all the energy flow and nutrition for the body, then the chakras must also supply the body with the messages from the brain that creates cause and effect. Then one must look at the location of each chakra's and what effect it is having on your mind, body, and spirit. Fear is the first step to dysfunction. Just for a moment close your eyes and imagine your spine. Take three deep breaths and focus on your feelings, see if you can detect any blockages radiating from your spine. Be sure to write down in detail in your journal what you experience, and remember the answers are all in the detail. I cannot reiterate this enough.

Energy flow in someone experiencing acute trauma (such as being involved in a plane crash or something catastrophic) will have an immediate reaction and will develop lactic acid that will attach itself to the meridian grid of the body and the chakra that is closest to the area or emotion that was evoked by the trauma. It will almost always create acute immediate pain. Most individuals handle major traumas well and fall apart later. During the falling apart, the lactic acid will often dissipate rapidly or slowly, depending on the severity of the trauma. However, someone with long term, ongoing low grade repetitive trauma, such as day to day life in a dysfunctional system will hold on and hoard the lactic acid and store it as a body memory, sometimes permanently. The lactic acid will attach to the chakras located in the spine and cause mental and physical diseases.

The reason I selectively used the word system here is because it does not only have to apply to a family system. It can be your work system, friendship system, or a relationship system with others such as a child, sibling, co-worker, lover. (You get the picture). I want you to begin to look at all of your relationships and situations as a system. If you have trouble remembering, go back to chapter four, The Pecking Order. In the long run this may cause someone to create physical illnesses that can become life-threatening, thus confirming the belief that the leading cause of death in the U.S. is stress-related illnesses that are created from long low grade reoccurring trauma.

Let us look at the chakras again, what emotions govern them, and how those emotions affect the body, mind, and spirit. Now let us look at the root of things. When one thinks of a tree, one usually thinks of a large, strong sturdy and often old tree. The tree has always been associated with family. After all, one refers to their family history as the family tree. Why and how this came into being I don't know. My thoughts are that it was the only association someone could think of that represented strength and goes on forever and ever and ever and ever (get the point or should I just finish the book with goes on for ever and ever nonstop). The other, which I think, is the most important reason for referring to the family as a family tree, is the fact that there are some trees that have strong deep roots and are secured to the ground. In other words, one would say they are well grounded. The trees that are well grounded in a family tree are sturdy, dependable, rooted in tradition (getting the generational theme yet?) This of course does not matter if the sturdy roots are functional or dysfunctional. You see the important factor with this family tree is that no matter what the family as a system is, it would take a tremendous storm or someone in the system to go severely against the roots to make the tree weaken and fall.

On the other hand, there are trees that have shallow roots and because of the shallowness of the root, the family is easily uprooted. The tree with the short roots however shows no partiality to function or dysfunction. It is simply more venerable to change, but can be re-planted to also go on forever and ever. So with all that said, let's look at the root chakra located at the base of the spine.

This is what grounds one to the earth and the basis one builds their house on so to speak. It is also the location that becomes affected first by low grade trauma that can happen to an individual in their adult life or even in childhood (such as finances, divorce, loss of a love or livelihood, moving, death of a pet, not feeling loved and accepted for one's self, and finally the worst underlying one that all the others bring on is the feeling of abandonment). So when the root chakra flow is interrupted by low-grade trauma, a chain of events begin to occur.

First, the brain alerts the root chakra the nature and cause of the low grade trauma is, ABANDONMENT. The next link in the chain that occurs is for the body to tense up and begin to produce lactic acid which attaches itself to the meridian grid in the body that is located in the root charka. Then the body begins an excess production of Cortisol to calm the reward or pleasure center of the brain down, when the flow in that center is filled, the overflow of Cortisol goes on to the frontal lobe of the brain that controls obsessive thoughts and a cycle has begun.

Can you see how a tolerance for the pain of low-grade trauma can be built up over a period of time, especially if this occurred as a child, which in most cases it does? So one needs to know that the core, or the root if you will, for one's chosen problems in life are unresolved issues of abandonment.

It is too painful for one to simply jump in and say, I'm going to start and focus on my abandonment issues. This has to be led up to by resolving the issues that caused the abandonment and work one's way down to the root or core of the problem. Often times, individuals do not know that they have abandonment issues, so to go there first would be a mistake in more than one way.

The other way is that if the abandonment occurs in childhood, the brain was functioning at 10.5 cycles per second (Alpha) not the 20 or 21 cycles per second (Beta) that one is functioning at in their here and now moment. To remove the trauma completely out of one's life, one must re-write the trauma at the level of brain functioning it was created in. If not, the trauma will keep returning in the person's life over and over. It's funny how God will have a person's life repeat itself until the individual is back to being whole.

Therefore, to sum up the root charka, it is the base or root of one's life and is affected by the issues of abandonment. As the issues of abandonment are dealt with, the less disruption to the flow of energy within ones' system, and a lifestyle that one wishes to have will begin to occur for them. One can now move out of the wish phase into the desire phase where manifestation begins to occur.

The next vertebra of the spine, or the sacral chakra, is the chakra that affects sexuality. We now move from the root of abandonment to the loss of one's identity. When one detaches from the internal part of them that is connected to the power that is greater than oneself or God, an individual begins to deny one's own sexuality, believing they are not OK to be male or female. This can occur as a result of messages received at an early age and remember that early in life one is functioning at a brain wave cycle of 10.5 cycles per second. Therefore, the messages out of a parents mouths or anyone that is influential in one's life at that early age becomes gospel. It becomes set in concrete for example the overt abuse that may occur in a child's life can be inappropriate touching or in some cases actual sexual acts (incest is more common than one would believe). Incest or sexual abuse can occur from family members or adult friends of the family, a teacher, or even a stranger. Overt sexual abuse will often lead to eating disorders.

Covert sexual abuse occurs in one way or another to almost everyone, and can also lead to eating disorders, especially if the focus of the covert abuse was related to appearances. The covert abuse is non-discriminating and affects males and females equally. In fact, there is always a rise in males during times of stressors within the country, for example, when there is a war, and Dad has to go off to war, what is the most common statement the father will make to the male child or the eldest male child in the family? "Take care of your mother, sisters, and brothers while I am away. You are the man of the house now." How overwhelming is that for a young child to hear? Now they are being told to take on a role that sometimes even an adult has difficulty with. Alternatively, consider the widow or divorced single mom, whose male child in the family, as though through osmosis, takes the message that they have to become mom's surrogate husband and confidant. How about the girls that are trying to make peace between mom and dad when it comes to visitation, or what if she and her siblings are being raised by their father? They also, as if through osmosis, take on the wife role with dad and become the surrogate wife. This has been discussed in Wendy and Jack's story. For right now, I want you to just keep this in mind and, if you can, journal your thoughts of how that was for you in your family system (yes, that's right, in detail).

Overt sexual abuse can be so subtle that no one notices when it is being done. For example, how many of you remember their father or mother saying, "You aren't going out dressed up like that are you?" This statement is always accompanied with the parental look that the child translates as *there must be something wrong with my* identity. There is a saying that one often hears, if not at home, while out in a grocery store shopping. You might overhear a parent say to a male child (if they fell or hurt themselves and began crying), "Big boys don't cry."

These are ways one receives the covert messages that are absorbed by us as children and again, because the brain is operating at 10.5 cycles per second, it is taken as the truth. Which brings me back again to my abandonment theory: that one must go back to the brain wave cycle at which the trauma occurred to resolve the issue so that it will not come back to bite at the most inconvenient time.

The third chakra located in the solar plexus is associated with emotions - in other words, your gut reaction to things (do not try to tell me you have never had a gut reaction to something; you know what I am talking about). When one's emotions are affected, it will automatically make an individual become defensive and create an acute self-esteem issue, (which a lot of us walk around with all our lives, either off and on, or all the time). This is the area that says to you, "You are not good enough" and as with all of the chakras, the energy flow will be disrupted causing one to get stuck and unable to get out. It is also this vertebra chakra that spurs on the adrenal glands to begin production of the stress hormone cortisol. So the cycle begins: *there is something wrong with me, I must have done something wrong to cause this, I must be a bad person, no one loves or cares about me or my problems.* We are not only back to the point of *a band on me*, we are also back to an over production of cortisol, and the obsessive thought process is in full swing.

Are you beginning now to see how this is all connected? Moreover, can you see how if one vertebra or chakra is off, it will affect the entire system (again with the system; I really want you to get that word in your head for later down the road, because it too, creates and perpetuates the cycle of self-sabotage).

The fourth chakra is connected to the heart or if you will the feeling of being loved or being in love. I would like you take a few minutes and write (in detail) in your journal what love means to you. I would like to challenge you to keep an open mind and make no judgments, good or bad, because there is no good or bad, there simply is.

The most important statement I want you to understand is this one:

Love does not hurt.

If it hurts, it is something else (like codependency or abandonment wounds).

Some people say they love with their head and some with their heart. I believe that one loves with their beliefs, here is why.

The formula goes something like this Love = Home. Whatever you learned from your childhood environment is what you look for and attract to you, functional or dysfunctional. For example, if Mom and Dad expressed themselves by verbal abuse to each other, but never left each other, the message one might get is that love = verbal abuse of each other and no matter what you do, do not leave. Having grown up with this the internal statement to one's self might go like this, "I will never have a relationship like my parents had." This would be especially true if as a child this was painful to watch and created a great deal of pain, as this would serve to reinforce the feelings of abandonment.

You see, children do not have the ability to filter out the difference between reality, emotion, functional, or dysfunctional, and that the issues are between Mom and Dad. They think, "Mom and Dad would not be abusive to each other and love would not hurt if I was better." Children believe that somehow they are the cause, and think if only I could change and be better (whatever they perceive that to be). They may even try to change Mom and Dad through trial and error, with their own behaviors. The problem is that there will always be error, because it has nothing to do with them.

You see, we instinctively know that love does not hurt, because at that early of age one is still connected to their God. The lines between God and parent's beliefs are becoming blurrier and blurrier and with the continual messages they are receiving from Mom and Dad, they are almost, but not completely broken - but they might be hanging by a thread. All they know is that what is going on in their home does not feel good.

It is at this point that one sets out to find someone completely different from Mom or Dad. They find someone that will not even raise their voice and think they have found their perfect mate. They get married, live together, and develop this pattern in all relationships in their lives, such as friends. They may even get a job where co-workers are non-abusive. After a while, because the stress is not there for them like it was when they were a child, the decrease in the stress hormone cortisol begins to create a craving, and they will begin to attempt to create chaos in order to get others in their life to act out so that the hormone will begin production and they will feel normal. (Sound like addiction? It should.) This in turn affects the chakras, the body responds by developing lactic acid, and a body memory is formed. This cycle serves two purposes for the individual:

1. It helps one maintain what one feels is normal to them.

2. If one can change and make this relationship right it will make one's growing up OK and mom and dad's problem will be solved. Then one can begin to believe things in their life were not an illusion. It was really love.

I would like you to stop right here and research your messages about love in your family, (in detail in your journal). Be honest. The only one you will hurt if you aren't, is yourself. I understand that this is often the place where a lot of people get stuck. Remember the goal and the reasons you picked up this book in the first place, and walk through the fear. Remember it is not the fear you are afraid of, it is the consequences of fear that you are afraid of. The answer is yes, it will bring into question your current relationships. If this instills fear, just know this is triggering your issues of abandonment and the only one that can abandon you is yourself. We came into this world alone, and we go out alone, therefore we are whole alone!

The fifth chakra, located in the spine behind the throat, is called the throat chakra, and affects one's ability to speak or be vocal. This chakra is almost always affected in the individual that comes from dysfunctional family systems, since the hard and fast rule of "don't talk, don't feel," and "you did not see what you thought you saw," and "you certainly did not hear what you think you heard." This is how one develops the inability to trust their own decisions and are sometimes referred to as a door mat in relationships. Often the individual will exhibit symptoms of problems with their vocal cords, laryngitis, or thyroid health issues. If the flow of this chakra goes untreated, some say it could even lead to throat cancer. There are often eating disorders as a result of this chakra's flow being disrupted. Others, as a rule, like these individuals because they tend to become people pleasers in order to not feel inadequate.

The sixth chakra is located in the spine directly behind and between the eyes. We are all intuitive. There is nothing magical about it. How many times can you walk into a room and instantly know and can read the temperature - whether the people are friendly and receptive or not. You sum all of this up, just walking into a room. This intuition is often referred to as reading the energy. Individuals are surrounded by an energy field. Think about it. There are times when you want to be left alone, and sure enough no one will approach you. There are other times you want to laugh and have a good time and people are attracted to. We control the energy that we send out to others. This is the way we learn to develop our boundaries without having to risk acceptance or rejection and not having to verbalize the need to move away, and say you're too close.

Individuals have four recognized zones in non-verbal energy expressed by individuals. Let us start with the closest to one's body. It is called The Intimate Zone which is 6 to 12 inches from another individual. This zone is often defined by one's family of origin's beliefs of the feeling of trust and safety. Individuals reserve this zone for personal friendships and sexual intimacy. The next zone is the Personal Zone, which is 36 inches or about arm's length. Entrance into this energy zone is normally by non-verbal invitation and is reserved for friends and close working relationships. Then there is the Social Zone which is 8 to 20 inches or the distance needed to be able to hear them speak. This is also determined on the social setting one is in and is often determined by the environment, and if it is noisy or quiet. When a person becomes aware that someone has entered their social zone, they generally feel inclined to interact with that person in some way. The fourth zone is the Public Zone and is usually beyond the limits of hearing. When an individual enters this zone, usually they do not exert any influence on the non-verbal behavior. They are viewed as part of the environment and require no special attention or recognition.

As mentioned previously, the sixth chakra is the intuitive chakra and is often referred to as the third eye, ESP, or conscious contact. Everyone has the ability to alter their energy vibrations in the brain through their thoughts. Think for a moment. Have you ever had a thought of a sad event in your life and your mood shifts from happy to melancholy? Have you ever thought of something happy, and realized that your mood has moved from melancholy to happy? (Of course you have). This is part of the intuition part of the brain. Let me ask you, have you ever had a premonition and have it come true? This is your intuition in action. The intuition is also related to the brain wave cycles and is accessed at a 10.5 cycle per second. Often this is referred to as the state of deep prayer, meditation, or conscious contact with God. Every individual has the ability to access this part of them, but it is often feared, primarily because of false beliefs about the change in consciousness. When this energy flow becomes unblocked, it will help you create the inner peace you are seeking in life. For right now, I would like you to stop again and journal about your feelings regarding your intuition.

Levels of boundaries are unconsciously developed from childhood messages about trust and comfort with intimacy. For example, have you ever experienced someone giving you a hug and you begin to pat them on the back almost immediately. Non-verbally you are thinking, "I don't know, or trust this person. Enough already with the hugging" If any kind of sexual overt or covert played a large role in an individual's life, often these individuals do not like to be hugged or touched. Then there are the extremes that begin to occur in others and because they cannot comfortable verbally express themselves they will act out with an addiction like sex or food.

The seventh chakra in located at the top of the head and even though it is not directly connected to the spinal column, it is the first chakra that intermediates between the power greater than ourselves, or God, as you understand him or her. This is where individuals feel the floating sensation when meditating or deep prayer. Did you know that this chakra is the one that is also associated with the dream or Alpha irrational energy of the brain and an individual experiences this as a natural occurrence every ninety minutes at night? This is what individuals that believe in ESP, psychics, and card readers get the information that they tell the future by. There are also those that fear this ability and believe that it is against good or somehow the devil can come in and take over.

The fact is everybody has this natural ability to connect with their higher power or God. If an individual is fearful of the devil, then the devil will appear. You have control of the connections you make and remember you cannot fear or receive into existence to something you do not believe in. Fear has a tendency to get in the way of our contact with God in order to avoid taking responsibility for ourselves and remain a victim in our own lives. This breads blame, resentments, and negative feelings that will cause one to spin their wheels and remain stuck in the negative patterns one has created for one self.

The eighth chakra is located above the head and is true spirit of life and the connection to all that exists. This is where one has access to each other's soul and is the connection to all of God's creations and God himself. This is the reason one draws the energy to live and move forward in life. It is the source of an individual's desires in life and is where it is believed an individual's destiny came into existence. It is also, where some believe the spirit exits the human body at death. This would support the Bibles statement that one must return as child to enter the kingdom of heaven. Which in turn would support that one must return to the 10.5 cycles of the brain vibration to resolve negative core beliefs. Is it not great how the universe continues to come together and form a perfect circle (or a band if you will) creating completion and always returning to Mother, Father, and A band on me. The universe also talks about balance between the sexes and the paradox of the differences.

Chapter 8

Are Relationships Just a Phase We Go Through That Will Affect Our Lives Forever?

Back to the wedding band, or *a band on me*

Love is a decision.

We forget that we make choices on how we are loved because we revert to the familiar:

Love = Home

instead of

Love = Choice + Decision on how we are loved

Now that we are back to the wedding band and the generational theory of A band on me, let us take a close look at how covert sexual abuse plays such a big part in the development of the core issues of dysfunctional beliefs of A band on me. I will be repeating myself throughout parts of this book, because major points deserve to be repeated: *Love does not hurt; if it hurts, then it is something else and making a commitment to the right person will liberate you; making a commitment to the wrong person will emotionally imprison you.*

With that being said, let's look at covert abuse. First, the female meets the male and they fall in love. Then comes marriage or commitment to be together, after entering the first stage of a relationship, which is...

Phase 1: The Honeymoon

This can last for a various amount of time depending on each individual. Once this phase is over the second phase begins.

Phase 2: Power Struggle

Most of us are familiar with this stage. This is the first time that what the partner does irritates the other and they confront them.

For example, one of them leaves the toilet seat up and the partner sits down and gets wet, or one of the partners squeezes the toothpaste tube and forgets to put the lid back on. After the conflict, makeup sex leads back to the honeymoon phase until the next power struggle occurs. Next comes phase three of the relationship:

Phase 3: Compromise

This is the one that is the most difficult for the one that needs to always be in control to work through, and it is at this phase that partners begin to look around for a way to bring the relationship back together.

So let us look at the reason most couples get married. Usually one grows up thinking that the thing that is a given is to grow up, get a good job, work on the career, then meet their perfect soul mate, and get married and have kids. The main thought that usually goes with that belief is that I will never raise my kids the way my parents raised me. This is the thought that crosses most couples mind whether or not they came from a dysfunctional family or not.

So now they are thinking that things are not as they were in the beginning. He/she is not the person I married. Maybe if we have children things will go back to the honeymoon stage and things will be the way I always thought my life would turn out to be. You saw how this played out in Wendy and Jack's story.

Now the first child has been born, and just as an example let us says the first-born is a girl. Watch how nature and God keep reinforcing for us that we must accept the masculine and feminine part of our selves. The words now change from husband and wife which has nothing to do with male or female to Mother and Father. The words now start with an M for male and F for female, thus making the statement again that one must accept the masculine and feminine part of ones' self, not someone else's self (get it? if not think about it will come to you).

Now, back to the covert sexual abuse and the making of an adult child of a family system. (I use family here because it is important to know that this is how functional relationships work as well. Whatever that is, as I personally have never seen a family without some type of dysfunction, but then it could be only people that need help for the dysfunction come to see me. Nah!). Now those of us that have had the awesome privilege to be blessed with a child (in this case let us say a female child). To make it real let's call her Kelly.

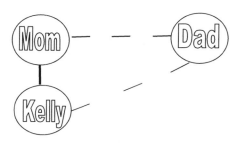

Kelly is your average baby (whatever that means), and she needs lots of attention at first.   Since children are totally dependent on their parent's or primary care giver in the first stages of life, Mom and often Dad are awakened at night to feed and change Kelly's diapers, and rock her if she has problems sleeping. This requires a lot of time for both parents.   Often exhausted, they sleep when they can. This is not the closeness they thought this baby would bring to the relationship. So gaps, if you will, begin to form between Mom and Dad. The distraction and the unconditional love that is developing between Kelly and her parents is causing more and more loss of intimacy between Mom and Dad. When Kelly starts going to school, Mom now has more time and will often return to work. Dad, who has never stopped working, begins to bond more and more with Kelly, since Mom is working long hours at work and around the house, and is often too exhausted to spend quality alone time with Dad. Dad and Kelly are now more bonded. Mom might feel left out and an unspoken rivalry between mother and daughter over Dad's affections. In order to make things work again the often-unconscious thought is that having another child will solve the problem.

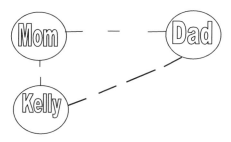

This is when covert sexual abuse occurs when Daughter becomes the surrogate wife to Father, having to take on the adult role of the wife. (Not necessarily any physical sexual acts occur, but can). If the physical act should occur, that is overt sexual abuse.

So Child number 2 is born, and this time it is a boy. Let's call him Robert.

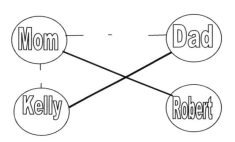

This is when covert sexual occurs when Son becomes the surrogate Husband to Mother, having to take on the adult role of the husband. (Not necessarily any physical sexual acts occur, but can). If the physical act should occur, that is overt sexual abuse.

So Robert is born and again it is back to the up and down nights and the no time for each other, and Kelly, because mom is busy with Robert, bonds more and more to Dad, causing more gaps between Mom and Dad. (Because we are meant to have a male half and a female half to be whole, and because Mom and Dad married to feel whole, the bonding repeats itself in reverse and Mom begins to bond more and more with Robert, thus creating a surrogate wife for Dad so he can feel whole and a surrogate husband for Mom, so she can feel whole).   Again, one is always looking for their missing piece in order to feel complete. This is a natural drive and occurs not out of dysfunction but out of nature in order for survival.

The dysfunction occurs from the wrong ways of seeking one's missing piece.   The effect on the children in this home then becomes, "I must not have needs. I now must meet the needs of my parents or no one will be there to help me survive." (You see this is all done out of the need for survival of each member of the family). This is covert sexual abuse and since it is a family or a marriage matter (remember the band? If not, go back and read, what is a band), this pain now becomes generational.   It is passed down for generations and generations until the pain of unconditional love becomes so intense that someone stops the cycle.

What is the source of <u>your</u> pain?

How many times have you had a pain in the neck, a headache or a backache not resulting from injury and never directly related it to your relationships with others?

The next time your head begins to throb or your neck starts to hurt ask yourself, "Who has been a pain in the neck lately? Who is affecting the very foundation of my life? Why does my head hurt?   Is my mind overloading from a bad relationship that forces me to think too much and feel too little or the other way around? If I have eyestrain, what is it I don't want to see? If I have an earache, what is it I don't want to hear? If I have a kidney infection, who am I pissed off at?"

The point is that you will begin to notice all the roles played throughout the book were used to demonstrate how these patterns are formed. It is the unbelievable the tolerance for stress that people develop. The sad part is, they don't even know that it is abnormal to be under this kind of pressure.

Seeing One's Theory Through Another's Eyes

As you know from my bio that I am a teacher and my students are studying for the State Testing for Chemical Dependency in the state of Texas. I feel that it helps individuals to pay more attention to a theory when given an example of the effects a theory has on other individuals. It is with this in mind that I was privileged to have a student give his views for me to print in hopes that it will help the readers understand that sometimes subtly can often times be the best teacher.

I gave my students an assignment to write a fairy tale and bring it to class in order to demonstrate how using fairy tales with clients can often be revealing. This is a copy of his writings. He has given me permission to share with my readers, along with the copy of his fairy Tale. Enjoy! He is very impressive and expressive in his writing (I am jealous).

First His Introduction

I have been a credentialed minister for seventeen years and during that time, I have had the privilege to counsel many people for a variety of issues. There are times counselors are so busy trying to direct hurting people to a better life they put away their own issues. Sometimes they think they have dealt with them but something will touch that painful memory and it rises to the surface. I am presently a LCDC student at The Institute for Chemical Dependency Studies in Houston, Texas. My instructor's name is Jayne Payne. Jayne has taken me for quite a journey not only in my education to become a counselor but a healing journey away from the self-destructing issues in my life. When I started the class, Jayne said that I would end up questioning everything that I thought I understood as truths. She was right. Using many different therapy techniques, I have faced many issues in my life and have accomplished great healing and understanding. Jayne uses her knowledge like a fisherman uses bait. She throws out a statement and pulls the class in with the hook deep in our thinking. Every student has had personal issues brought to the surface and skillfully directed not only on how to let them go but how to help other people. This journey that I call a class has opened my eyes to a whole new and exciting way of thinking and has brought a healthy lifestyle change in me.

From a Class Assignment to the Beginning of Healing

Once Upon A Time was always the beginning of a fairytale that I would read to my grandchildren, until the day I met Jayne Payne. What started out to be a class assignment turned out to be the beginning of a healing journey for me. Jayne is my LCDC class instructor and she gave the class an assignment to write a Fairy Tale. I didn't have any idea how writing a story would affect my life. I decided that I would base my story on Jayne's theory of abandonment. My Fairy Tale was about a man who started on a journey to search for some answers to his life. I reviewed my notes from class and started to have fun telling a story. As my story started to come together, I realized that the man I was writing about was me. By the time I was finished I understood her theory and for the first time in my life I could deal with the issues that have burdened me for so long.

-Jack Houston (student)

Jack's Fairytale

THE SPIRITUAL JOURNEY OF A MAN CALLED BETA 20.21

Once Upon A Time in a land not to far away in a city called Abandon me and in a time that felt like it would never end, lived a man called Beta 20.21 Beta 20.21 lived his life with much pain and dysfunction. He lived in the city of Abandon me his whole life, and for all of those years he hoped that his life would change.

He would do the same things day in and day out hoping for a change but nothing changed. He would wake up every morning believing his body would not have the same memories as yesterday but they were always there, this morning he arose up out of bed and felt the same covert abuse slapping him as he faced another day. Beta 20.21 felt detached from something his whole life; always in his mind he heard a voice telling him he was not ok. He was broken; not good enough. Beta 20.21 remembered that for three generations his family all felt the same way: that they were all cursed.

Beta 20.21 had obsessive thoughts about this trauma in his life and he finally said "I will not be manipulated by my core beliefs anymore". Beta 20.21 knew that he needed help to get from wishing he could change, to his desire for what was missing in his life. Beta 20.21 decided to go see the great philosopher and healer Enyaj Enyap, some say she had magic powers and a theory on how to change.

This woman lived in the Orient in a town called Meridian at the corner of Logical and Creative, right before you get to Spine Street. Beta 20.21 walked 12 steps into her fortress called Body, Mind, and Spirit and said, "I need a point of reference to find my faith." The great healer said that he needed to go to the City of Puberty were everybody believes everything and find a boy called Alpha 10.5. She said if he could get back to Alpha 10.5, he could be healed.

The great healer told Beta 20.21 that it would be a painful journey and his search for knowledge would take a great understanding guide named The Counselor to help him get there. The Counselor and Beta 20.21 went on their journey past the corner of Logical and Creative and thru the Masculine part of town but went around the Feminine part of town because The Counselor had issues with the people who lived there and was afraid of that area. As they journeyed through the City of Puberty Beta 20.21 if he heard him right, did he say he couldn't find him because Beta 20.21s body language was saying something else?

The Counselor summarized the situation and came up with a measurable and doable plan. The Counselor directed Beta 20.21 to meditate for 90 minutes and when he sees Alpha 10.5 he needs to focus for 17 seconds. The Counselor said if he did that he could change the family issues that have hurt him all those years. Beta 20.21 followed The Counselors directions and looked up, he could see a young boy around seven years old, and when the young boy turned around Beta 20.21 realized the he was the young boy. Beta 20.21 faced the issues that made him feel inferior and empty and separated from God and he finally realized what it was like not to live in The City of Abandon me. In Beta 20.21s new life, he traveled past the City of Puberty and The Land of Dysfunction and into a new time in his life. Beta 20.21 looked over his home and family, and then he smiled because he knew that the evil generational curse was broken and the demons were dead and he could enjoy the rest of his life, with his princes, his children, and grandchildren.

The End

--Jack Houston

Losses are required to grow

I read a book once about losses in life. Like all things that are truths in one's life, it depends on when you are exposed to the truths that will have a life changing impact on your life. I have had many of those of late and that is why I am adding this chapter to the book. I think life changing moments and new ways one begins to look at them, help one come together with the thoughts in one's head plus the emotions in one's heart and gut. Being an abstract thinker and using Albert Ellis theory, play it out in your mind to the extreme to obtain a grasp on what is really real, what is not, and if one's thoughts and feelings are valid or just made up to be what we want them to be to avoid the big A word ABANDONMENT.

Getting it Together

Now you are probably saying that is all well and good and maybe even interesting, but how does all of this cause me to self-sabotage. How can all of this help me make the changes and develop new beliefs that will help create the life I want? I know the suspense is getting to you, since almost everyone wants a quick fix---even though it took a lifetime to create the problem. Yes, you heard me right. You would like nothing better than to blame others for not getting what you want or why you can't have it. We would like to blame our life circumstances, mother, father, sister, brother, etc (You get the picture). However after the age of seven according to psychologists, the personality and all of our beliefs about life are in place, before one is able to determine for one's self what is right or wrong. You should be able to understand this even better having reading Chapter X, the Pecking Order. If you don't, go back and read it. There is a large resistance to accepting responsibility for ones' own life. The largest fear is that somehow we have failed. For some reason the word fail has a negative connotation. We all seem to forget that it is usually only after failure that success can occur. Alternatively, maybe it is success we really fear. Either way, it is the fear that keeps one stuck, or self-sabotaging. However, you will begin to understand in my theory and point of view, one can only fear something if they believe it has a reason to be feared (back to those old core belief issues again).

Chapter 9

Flush for Yourself, Not Others

The Increase in Detachment Disorders

There have been new trends that occur in this profession since the beginning. The newest one is that there is an increase in several mental health diagnoses as of late. There has been an increase in bipolar disorders, autism, and detachment disorders. It is detachment disorders that I would like to address. The internet has had an impact on everyone, however, again we have a tendency to blame rather than look at the cause. With the need for more families to have more than one member of the family work to support the family way of life and provide all of the things in life that is required to fill it when you feel half full, along with the need to work longer and harder, faith becomes secondary in the family life, thus causing each member to go off in different directions to look for their missing piece. With the internet and modern technology at one's finger tips , escape becomes easy, and with the safety to be able to maintain anonymity on line, individuals can escape in many directions to attempt to fill the emptiness not being met in the way God intended it to be. It affects the young as well as the old, because it is generational and thus, is passed down.

When abandonment, or abandonment wounds, occur at an early age, when boundaries, the basic beliefs, and emotions are established, this is the true cause of detachment disorders. Being detached from one's self and God is the point of abandonment. It is impossible to attach to others, until one is first attached to one's self. The resolution to become aware and take responsibility to reconnect to one's higher self through, the process of grief from all of life's losses, it becomes next to impossible to stop self-sabotage and become whole, finding one's missing peace.

A Simple Explanation of Mental Health Labels

Diagnosis vs. Disorder

Today the individual has been ignored and we have started categorizing and labeling whatever the new trend, catchy name, and specific symptoms. So now everyone can find their label by going to any self help book or just asking your doctor, what am I according to the DSMR on the new revised version. After all, new names and categories are invented almost every week. Next week you can be something else like codependent one day and love avoidant the next. Why can't we just say we are wounded from childhood with dysfunctional beliefs that separates us from God?

Let me start at the beginning. How does this work in the field of therapy and psychology in as simple of terms as I can. First, in the field, you have what is called a "Mental Health" diagnosis, and then you have what is known as disorders.

Mental Health is considered treatable because it is medicateable, a big word for controllable through the use of medications that help control the symptoms of Mental Health diagnosis like bipolar, schizophrenia, autism, etc. There are medications that can help with some of the symptoms, not all of them mind you, but enough that it becomes safer and more comfortable for all concerned. Doctors are not sure what actually causes the mental health diagnosis. What they do know is that it can be genetic (passed down in a family, or for some unknown reason a chemical imbalance in the brain like neurotransmitters and receptors inability to send the correct messages to each other, like with the Cortisol and drug affected brain.

Either way, science says again, let's stop the symptoms and look at the cause, .for the diagnosis. So the answer is medicate/control them. If there is money left over, then research and explore the cause and see what we can do. Notice no mention of prevention. There is such a relief from the quieting of the symptoms and research is so expensive and pharmaceutical companies do not wish to go there with their money (Wonder why?) It is far better to focus on medication research than possible prevention. This is not just true with mental health. It is also true with medicine in general and goes back to human nature, "give me a quick fix. I can't stand the pain." (Sorry my soap box again.)? This stance has often made me unpopular and often challenging in my own field. It is never easy swimming upstream with sharks behind you; especially if you don't know how to swim. **If you are reading this book and have one of these diagnoses or know someone that does, I would like to stop swimming for a minute to say. I never recommend anyone getting off of any prescribed medications without a doctor's consent, as it could be harmful even life threatening to yourself or others.** However, always look for the cause, no one is going to be a better advocate for you than you and maybe Susan Summers. Can't wait for when she turns from physical health to mental health or just maybe she will find the link. I am sure there is one! Scientists are beginning to explore the possibility that some of this is genetic and passed from generation to generation thus, "The sins of our father's, from the bible, that's right back to Adam and Eve, but wait if we were created in God's image did he have sins too and are we doomed to be locked into abandonment and wandering around in the desert for 40 years. Maybe that is why we don't come into our own until we hit the magic age of 40. OH well, passed that (Been there done that) Nothing profound happened (except some of my body parts went south). Just food for thought, and further, more when we ignore God does he feel abandon by us? I bet he knows how to heal at 10.5 cycles per second in the brain! After all, we were given a clue when it was said of Jesus. These things I do you can do and more.

Now, where was I? Oh, yeah, exploring. Now there is some evidence that a majority of mental health diagnosis is somehow related to dysfunctional family systems, but doctors are unable to determine which came first (the chicken or the egg)? Sorry, I mean dysfunction or mental health. To look at that one might have to acknowledge one's own family dysfunction unless the researcher is the "Normal One" at which point I want to know who designated them normal, because I want to be normal too. This is why my interest in medical is short and cynical. Coming from my dysfunctional system, by the time I would complete training, I would have every diagnosis and symptom known to man and then some. Not that dysfunctional systems lead to detachment, addiction, and disorders...or DO THEY?

Now, I will get back to the task at hand and in simple terms attempt to explain "Disorder". I am convinced there are as many disorders as there are out-of-order restrooms in the world. I would like to talk first about the meaning of the word "Disorder". When you first see it taped to the stall of the restroom (Yes, I am going somewhere with this). Your first thought might be "someone who was uncaring of others and their needs. For someone stuffed the toilet full of paper and caused it to back up and not flush, no one ever thinks that this person who stopped up the toilet with paper might be a person who cares about me so much that they put too much paper in the toilet so that it would be extra clean for me when I want to use it and that maybe, just maybe, this was an act of unselfish love and caring on the individuals part. Now I know you are asking yourself right this minute, How does she have the time to stand outside the out of order stall and think of all of these thoughts? Well it is easy, because I am like you waiting in line to use the one that is not out of order. You know the one that has been neglected by a detached individual who needs no one to send them an e-mail to thank them for their thoughtfulness.

OOPS, back to the paper. Maybe the paper can be used as a symbol of the overly codependent family system that keeps shoving all of the dysfunction crap at you until one chokes or just stops functioning at all. Until one day a psychiatrist looks at them and says you have a "disorder", and therapy is prescribed. So, like Drain-O® you are therapied...until your pipes are clean. The only problem with that is, unless the pipes have been cleaned at 10.5 cycles of the brain, one will seek out someone else to stuff them full of paper "disorder" again. This is why scientists say "Disorders" are incurable. So now let us look at dissociative disorders vs. detachment disorders. Even though some would say they are different. I beg to differ, there I go again begging see how easy it is to slip back into old patterns and ways? But becoming aware and taking responsibility can become almost automatic, if the core issues of abandonment are addressed at the 10.5 cycles of the brain. So to restate my own opinion, dissociative and detachment disorders are one and the same. The definition in mental health fields is that to have a dissociative disorder one must have experienced a trauma such as abuse or traumatic happening in one's life, and the disassociation is an attempt to avoid something that is so painful for one to handle-instead of looking at it from the standpoint that to dissociate is an automatic and natural way for one to survive. Every human has the ability to dissociate at any time for any reason, even the "normal ones" as well.

Let me explain ... Have any of you ever just sat and daydreamed of better times? How many of you pray or meditate daily? Well, when you do these things, you are functioning at 10.5 cycles of the brain. Why is this important? I am glad you asked. [If you didn't ask then skip this part.] Because science says that disassociation is a disorder, and I am saying that dissociation is in order. When one is in a dissociative state, one can, and often does, detach from one's own personal emotions and physical feeling and acknowledgements, thus spontaneous healing. It is through and only through disassociation and detachment that one can connect directly with his or her God. And it is at this

10.5 cycles does healing of all things occur and one can connect to an unbiased answer to questions and contact with a source of energy, vibration, or awareness that nothing is impossible. It is at the point that we re-attach to the conscious that belief begins to falter. Therefore, I believe that this is not a negative, but a positive order that can and does often lead someone back to sanity in a disordered world.

In a twelve step program like Al-anon the term often used is detach with love. Often that is mistaken for shove more paper in as they cannot possibly know how much to use on their own. A true Al-Anon that has done their own work on the core abandonment issues at the 10.5 cycles of the brain would hand you the toilet paper roll and say I trust your judgment and if you chose not to do it my way, I will not feel abandoned by you and when you take the gift having completed your own work on the core issues of abandonment at 10.5 cycles of the brain, you can feel free to accept the roll of paper or get your own, without fear of being abandoned or abandoning others in your life.

Remember fear is simple protection of false events appearing real. My point is that if everyone would not have to stand in line, thinking I hope it will flush easily for me so that the next in line can have clean pipes that don't require drain o, they would have clean pipes and things would flush easier for them in life. This, if you have not figured it out by now is how one can stop the generational cycle: It is only through disorder and detachment from one's self can one re-attach to order, which is God if you choose to think of it that way.

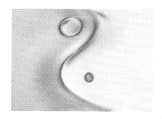

Disorders give us an opportunity to seek God and heal.

Disorders serve a purpose - to lead us back to God and be whole.

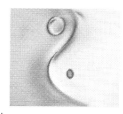

The truth will set you free.

Isn't that true for everyone? When faced with our personal truths, we are free to make a choice which is an original gift from God.

Freedom of choice, making one's own healthy choice, not the dysfunctional one we learned, creates our personal power in our lives.

Reconnecting with God allows the healing of unconditional love of ourselves. We accept and connect to the perfection of God within ourselves unconditionally. That's what makes us whole.

It's the LAST Frontier: Embracing Oneself and Reconnecting to God

(BREAKING THE CYCLE OF PAIN AND GRIEF)

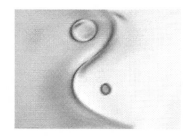

It's the giving up of the illusions and fantasies and seeing the truth that reconnects us to God.

For in this process we discover God never left us.

We left Him.

Chapter 10

Abandonment Wounds- The Last Chapter

If you don't have it by now read the book again

Self-abandonment is all about when your detachment from God occurred in your life. It is not about did it occur, or if it occurred. It is about when it occurred. Because you see, if you are reading this book, it occurred for you.

The solution to reattachment to God is about self-love, for if you can't love yourself, how can you love or acknowledge God? Notice, I did not say other people who you might perceive as more lovable or greater than yourself. Also notice I did not say unconditional love because there is no such thing as unconditional love. There is only acceptance.

Conditions are always put on us when it involves love: I love you because, or if you will, or if you do this. Conditions come not only from ourselves and others in our lives, it also comes from God himself. You must obey the Ten Commandments or else. From parents, you must bring home good grades, and from yourself, I must succeed or else. We put conditions on our own love of self. There are always or else's when unconditional love is in involved. However it never seems to stop each and every one of us from pursuing unconditional love. If we did not feel the self-abandonment we would not seek unconditional love at all. We would not need it. It would appear to us as self-acceptance.

Therefore, I prefer today to seek out self-acceptance and approval of myself in my life. This helps keep me focused on my goals and avoiding self-abandonment and detachment from the source that connects me to all things. There is a lot of scientific research that proves the theory of self-abandonment, but nothing proves this theory more than the emptiness someone feels when experiencing the emotions of the aloneness that bears the deafening sound of silence and the aching in your gut that will not be quieted nor soothed.

To understand why I make the statement that unconditional love does not exist, let us turn to facts and explore the definition of the words themselves, our fascination with them, and what we learned to believe they mean. Then we will explore what a relationship is, to explore if the two are even related. Finally, we'll look at God and the myth that his love is unconditional and heals all. Sometime he needs to leave us in pain of our abandonment wounds so that we may grow.

According to Webster's New World Dictionary, the definition of unconditional is the following: without conditions or reservations: absolute.

To love without conditions has already been determined in this chapter as an impossibility of our selves, others in our lives, and God himself. So therefore, unconditional has to be deleted from our need to be loved unconditionally. Leaving us with I just need to be loved.

In truth it cannot exist according to Webster. Is it really love that we are looking for in others? Well again, that is speculative according to our definition that we were brought up to believe what the word love means and for each of us that is a different meaning. So if none of us has the same meaning, how do we determine if someone does or does not love us? Being torn is what causes some of the pain of not feeling loved comes from. The other is one's own belief of what love equals and that someone does not live up to those expectations.

Let's look first at what Webster's says the definition of love is then I will attempt to explain how we come to believe what love is to us independently.

According to Webster's New World Dictionary:

Love: 1. Strong affection or liking for someone or something **2.** a passionate affection of one person for another **3.** the object of such affection; a sweetheart or lover **4.** Tennis a score of zero vt., vi. To feel love (for) - in love feeling love – make love 1. to woo, embrace, etc. 2. to have sexual intercourse – lov'able or lovea-ble adj – love'less adj.

Love'bird (burd) n. any of various small, old world parrots often kept as cvage birds love'lorn' adj. Pining from ove'ly adj. -lier, -li-est 1. beautiful 2.(colloq.) highly enjoyable – love'liness n. lov--er (luv'ar) n. one who loves; specif., a) a sweetheart b) a paramour c) (pl) a couple in love with each other d) a devotee, as of music love seat a small seat sofa for two people lov'ing adj. Feeling or expressing love – lov'ing-ly adj. Loving cup a large drinking cup with two handles, often given as a prize.

Wow what a definition. If you are not confused just by Webster's definitions alone, in just one word, love equals strong affection for someone or something passionate affection object of such affection, a game of tennis, and a score of zero (how does that make you feel about love being the same score as that of tennis and a zero at that?) The true definition of co-dependency old world parrots that are kept in a cage to pining for love that is on one hand highly enjoyable, a small sofa for two to a large two handled trophy cup given as a prize. Well, if that doesn't make you feel unconditionally loved I don't know what will.

God the final Chapter in the Universe or God the Final Stage of Growth

This book will end where it started and at the same juncture. There is something greater than myself that guides my life. Some call it fate, some call it destiny. I call it God. You can call it what you like. After all, words are just terms of endearment for our thoughts and feelings, each one of us wishes to express

Radical thoughts to ponder

> Unconditional love is loving someone enough to abandon them so that they can learn how to love and live and get back home to God.

It is human nature to always want to know the source of things that affect our lives. The source of our abandonment is one of those things. If one truly believes we are part or one with God, and we were sent here in this time and space by God to experience life lessons, then being sent from our origins would be the original point of abandonment for all of us.

Thus, the disconnection from our source occurred even pre-conception and increased in intensity. Abandonment keeps adding on to the pain of loss and rejection with each abandoning event that occurs in our lives. Like an onion layer upon layer adding up with each abandonment, bonding to the last layer creating a thin film of pain, when it is time to be peeled away. It is almost impossible to think that God would abandon us, but even on the cross, Christ cried out, "Why have thou forsaken me?"

Some might say that's a rhetorical question and that he was really asking himself *why have I abandoned myself.* It can be interpreted as him not pushing his Ego to express his beliefs. Could it be that one's beliefs could be dysfunctional as well, expecting a God who created abandonment to rescue us on the birth of our demise and the discovery? I use the words of demise and discovery because you can only discover your truths through the demise of your old dysfunctional thoughts, feelings, beliefs, ego, and death and rebirth. The perfect contact from our unconscious place of origin to the consciousness of whom and where we are today, thus making God the reality of what he wants for us today.

If abandonment was originated in us first by God this explains perfectly well why one must return to the original source for one's ultimate solution and peace to one's problems. Let us ask another question, is abandonment really a problem or have we created a problem out of abandonment? Life is full of necessary losses and most of the fears developed around those losses are distortions of ones imagination of the consequences that may or may not occur in our lives as a result. Thus, is fear of abandonment been created in much the same way?

Fear is a defense mechanism we use to paralyze ourselves to avoid moving forward in life. Instead, I like to look at the reason fear was originated for us by God. Fear was never meant to paralyze us it was simply a warning sign to move forward with caution, focusing on the results of the forward movement rather than the past. It is like the story of Lot in the Bible in turning to look to the past she became a pillar of salt frozen and stuck for all time. From birth to death there is but one path with no turning back; for at that point of death, one turns toward home and the Creator, embracing the original abandonment and ultimate reward of healing.

We are given glimpses of this experience in life. For without the issues of pain that abandonment creates, one would never so briefly experience the feeling of wholeness and healing that one will get in the end when closure of abandonment occurs. So embrace your issues of abandonment that have been created for you throughout your journey and the glimpses of your Creators glory will be shown on earth, creating for you the peace that you seek not the piece you have created and have been chasing in your life.

Standing at the kitchen sink, think about the new house that has been created around you with a window overlooking a beautiful pool, movers struggle to place the large statue of the Trojan horse you have purchased to remind you ,that sometime what is within, is stronger and can win over what is without.   A tremendous splash goes unnoticed by you . The movers have dropped your Trojan horse into the pool. Later, when relaxing by the pool, you see the horse submerged. How and when did that happen?

When surrendering to the facts, rather than attempting to control the fact it occurs to you the truth is the fact. That a big splash often goes unnoticed externally, but like the story of the Trojan Horse, internally submerged somewhere in the unconscious mind ever present, is the connection that has the power to heal. We come in alone, we go out alone, therefore we are whole alone, but we have a choice to be alone or not throughout the journey, and choice is more freeing than neediness.

The Faith to Heal

Now that the stories of Wendy and Jack's families have been told and hopefully related to how our family stories unfold in our lives and the generational results to come and the role that abandonment plays out in one's life, the service behind abandonment, and the hopefully provoking thoughts behind issues of abandonment, have started your wheels turning in your mind. One might ask: Now, that I know all of this and can relate, how does one heal? Well the answer is simple. The work is hard the rewards are worth it and the results are a reconnecting with God.

Step one: You have already begun through reading this book, you have become aware.

Step two: You are now ready to become responsible.

Step three: Hopefully, you have started taking that responsibility by creating a daily journal, identifying your daily self-abandonment actions, again becoming aware and taking responsibility for how often and under what circumstances you self-abandon.

Step four: Write down in detail how you self-abandon and how it made you feel.

Step five: This step is about change. One can only begin to change through purging, through prayer, meditation, and sharing one's truth's with others— regardless if they agree or accept your truth's for themselves. This simply means, share of yourself what is true for you, and begin to live by that truth. Then your life will serve as an example, letting others share their truth's without judgment. This is a demonstration of the strength of your connection with God and will serve as truth to the universe and God.

LOVE IS WHAT HOLDS THE KEY TO FREEDOM.

GOD IS PURE LOVE

To not risk giving or receiving love out of fear of being hurt is what detaches us from God (higher power) and creates spiritual bankruptcy and prevents us from recovery from our abandonment wounds.

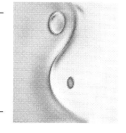

> *When we have the courage to look at our core hurts and grieve them at a deep level, we make room for healing. Our mind, body, and spirit rejoice.*
>
> *We can better live in the present moment and have a joyful heart, in and despite any circumstance, because we know where we come from and where we are going.*
>
> *We can then transcend in little and big ways and make our life into a gift to others.*

So there you have it. Do with it what you will. Just remember:

The final stage in almost any self-help and spiritual awakening book, the Big book of all 12 step programs, and the biggest book ever written, the Bible, says, "Go forth and spread the Word, share the message." I hope that you will.

This has always been my mission.... to help others that are in pain so they can start their journey to healing. I hope that you will join me in my peace, one person at a time, trusting that your mission of healing shows others there is a way out of the pain. There is a lot of peace to be had, and there is a place available to get it, and that is you.

Peace and love. –Jayne Payne

****

Today, I choose to risk loving and being loved. I open my heart and I am willing to heal. I walk through the fear of wounding others and myself, so that I can connect with God and achieve my highest good, to love others, and receive love from others in return. I choose to heal my abandonment wounds. I choose to live my life in the freedom of recovery.

Affirmation:

Chapter 11

Pre-boarding the Encounter

(Boarding the ship with the Intensive)

Jayne Payne talks about the negative tapes we hear. Those voices that play (many times the ones we heard growing up and the ones we've added along the way) are ways we self-abandon. Mine could be saying, "A book with Jayne? Who do you think you are? What do you have to say?" After walking my path, and believe me, I crawled for a long time searching for some relief, I am forever grateful that this tape is not playing. But, I think the who am I part serves a good purpose in beginning this section of the book: Book with Jayne.

It's the best title for this section because it's an inside look into my journey of, like this book has explained, realizing there is no missing piece, that abandonment wounds are real and affect our lives, that one can learn to not abandon oneself, that inner peace is there for the taking, that healing of abandonment wounds is possible, that the cycle is breakable, and that God never abandons us. We just have to seek him out and reconnect to Him and inner peace can once again reign in our soul.

Who am I? I am the daughter of Roberto Bucio, a retired steel machinist. A father that longs to be in his mother's arms, feeding her ripe strawberries as she lay, dying of cancer in Las Lomas near Michoacan, México. A man, the first of eleven brothers and sisters, who stayed in the United States so that his two daughters could pursue a career of their choice.

I am the daughter of Maria Luisa Bucio, a housewife that has dedicated her adult life raising my younger sister and me. A mother that longed her father to say Perdóname, te quiero mucho (Forgive me, I love you very much)—a phrase that I have witnessed firsthand the devastating effects that it can have on a daughter not to hear. The ripple effects of a physically and emotionally abusive father are potentially toxic. My mom, the second of five brothers and a sister, stayed in the United States so that her daughters could pursue their dreams and have the opportunities that she didn't have growing up.

I am a wife that has not been easy to live with. I was very needy. A wife that struggled with trusting and couldn't ask for what she needed. I didn't know how. I was in victim mode for many years. I was a wife that was quick to blame my immediate family for my discontent, chaos, and worries—my husband and my sons.

I am a mother that struggled to respond patiently and lovingly to our two sons. A mother that had the best of intentions to be a nurturer to her children, but anger and impatience got in the way.

I was a workaholic. I kept busy. I was a bilingual teacher, I had self-published reading and writing materials, and I documented my instructional practices and gave professional development in school districts. But somehow I felt that my personal life (my daily life with my husband and sons) was in shambles. It was out of control. I was not happy.

I am a child of God. I'm called to become a better version of me and am learning from all those who I have a relationship with, for they are teachers that help me on my path returning Home.

I had been raised in a wonderful home. My parents had taken good care of me, put my education as a top priority, trusted me, had sacrificed so much for my sister and I. I had not the faintest idea that what had put me in the state I was in, in 2006 when I was at my worst, had a lot to do with my family system growing up. I would later learn that because I wasn't aware of this, yet alone doing something about it, I was repeating the cycle and my children were also growing up in similar dysfunction. How could I be a nurturer to our two sons if I was in deep inner pain, depressed, anxious all the time, exhausted, angry, just to name a few things in my reality?

More specifically, I felt my husband was distant, my sons were a handful at ages three and six-months, and I didn't know it then, but I had depression and anxiety. I was miserable. I didn't feel I had much to give and I wasn't receiving much. I was exhausted. I was in despair and angry and tired and wanted my husband to somehow make my life better by being who I wanted him to be- by doing what in my mind meant love. He didn't. I felt let down. I felt stuck. This is not the life I wanted, I thought. One night, I was alone with the kids. I reached out to my Dad and I was talking to him how I wanted out. I couldn't see myself in the marriage anymore and I wanted my peace back.

One night that same week I was talking to my sister on the phone, sharing how all my problems were because of my husband and how hard it was to have peace and quiet raising the boys and on and on. She began crying for me and my situation, my unhappiness, and my version of my chaos. I was so out of touch with all other emotions but anger. And it was everyone around me, but me, that I looked at. As I heard the grief and sadness in her voice, I got a glimpse into the notion that I needed help. That, if I couldn't see it, but my sister, whom loves me and wants the best for me, saw it, then I needed to take action and find the help I needed. What I was doing was not working.

That night, this initial glimpse of awareness would gradually evolve and lead to today.

The first therapist I saw was in December of 2006. Towards the end of our session she asked me to see my doctor so I could get what I needed to help me feel better and less anxious and depressed. I was stunned and confused. I kept asking, "How will he know that that's what I need?" I remember her insisting that I make the appointment before Christmas and the offices close.

It was about five days to Christmas Eve. I remember asking my mom, "How could she have known I needed medication?" Looking back, of course I had anxiety. I was a wreck! I was depressed and had been for a very long time.

By the time I met Jayne, in April of 2009, I had seen four therapists in a period of a little over two years and by this time I was reading Codependency No More by Melody Beattie. Not only was I reading it, but I had started a book club with some close family members. Page after page, I related with what she described. There was a name to the frustration and loneliness and resentment that I harbored. I'm codependent, I thought. It's an amazing feeling, one of validation I guess, to learn you are not the only one that gets stuck in vicious cycles. It was relief to know that I was not the only one that got to a point in which I had to declare, "I am powerless and my life is unmanageable." It was so eye-opening and I grabbed onto its teachings for dear life!

The day I met Jayne in person, at one of her lectures, was a decisive moment in my life that ultimately leads to these pages. She had met my aunt while they were both getting a pedicure and Jayne had given my aunt her card and explained she was a therapist. Since we were in the book club and so many issues were coming up during our meetings, my aunt mentioned the book we were reading and the plan was for me to contact Jayne. When she gave me her card, I didn't see why that was necessary. I didn't have intentions to call. The next Sunday at the book club meeting, I felt so rattled and wounded and resentful with my mom that a desire to contact Jayne rose to the surface.

Both my aunt and I were at her next lecture. The room was packed, there were people sharing their experiences in the Intensive, and I felt like I had found what I was missing. I had found what I had been searching for. I thought I was just going to hear a lecture on abandonment, but that same evening, I had made a check to be in her next Intensive weekend. It was in two weeks. When it came right down to it, I had no idea what to expect, but the testimonials I heard at the lecture manifested that it was intensive and that it was worth doing. Not happy with my progress—it wasn't fast enough—I felt hopeful that the Intensive would get to the core issue that had me stuck. I write this because that's what I had learned in her lecture. Any type of trauma, low grade or ongoing trauma, gets us stuck.

When I met Jayne, I just knew that I had no choice. I had to sign up and do this. This could be it. I was reading, I was journaling, I would apply what therapy was teaching me, but I didn't feel well. My life felt shattered. I didn't feel I was in a loving relationship—at least my husband wasn't doing what I thought he should be doing to show me affection. By this time I had a five year old and a three year old son and I felt I couldn't keep up with all that required to take care of them and work and the writing I was doing…. I simply couldn't handle it. I felt so, so desperate. I didn't feel I had anything emotionally to give, and I was sure not getting what I wanted. I was tired. So, so tired.

The following is what I typed up in full a few days later after hearing Jayne speak. Knowing what you now know about Heroes, you will believe me that I have this glued onto one of my notebooks. I kept the entry just as I wrote it. I was as retrospective as they get during this time. I wanted to get better so desperately, and I became a professional analyzer and documenter:

I am mad. I want to express my frustration…as it has unfolded after hearing Jayne Payne share her theory on self-abandonment. She started talking why we seek professional help, what 'a band on me' means, why we look for someone/something to make us whole, and its connection to our family of origin, self-sabotage, shame, guilt, codependency, disconnection from God, how we end up abandoning ourselves, how are thoughts, feelings, and behaviors come from our family, if and how we operate out of need, the natural hormone cortisol and how we are physically addicted to it and have developed a high tolerance to it; and the brain waves we operate in (beta, alpha, theta, and delta), lactic acid crystals in our nervous system that become body memories, and how they are linked to physical disease. Like I said, more than what I could process or handle right now...but it made sense....two hours of aha! moments I couldn't stop her and tell her no, I don't identify with that.

Why am I mad? Because I understood things beyond me...from a different perspective and feel there were missed opportunities to get certain feedback from my past therapists...What did I know before hearing Jayne Payne? Based on my discoveries in therapy, reading <u>Codependent No More</u>, this is my synopsis. (I know, I know, bear with me).

1. Recognize when I'm reacting, allowing someone or something to yank my strings.

2. Make myself comfortable. For the present moment, to acknowledge and accept circumstance, myself, and others as they are

3. FEEL: Know that real power comes from feeling our feelings

4. EXAMINE WHAT HAPPENED: Tell myself the truth about what happened.-REALITY CHECK- Ask: Is my thinking rational? Am I having expectations? Do I need to change the thought? (and go down the list of questions).

5. Figure out what I need to do to take care of me. (depend on myself and PROBLEM SOLVE; self-love. Respond appropriately to my feelings. Make decisions based on reality and in a peaceful state (out of acceptance and gratitude). It is a place found in peace and trust, not urgency and intensity.

When you find a tool that works, you don't let it slip away. It becomes your temporary life jacket. Beattie's book and its gems were my life-jacket in that moment in time. I was exhausted of feeling overwhelmed and caved in. The therapy and the book club was part of my relief. I worked at it so I could make it my own and move forward. This is what it took for me to manage my days...to manage my sadness, my anger. Did I resent that I had to work so much to just feel a little better and handle my days? I did. My classic response to my therapist was to ask, "Why do I have to do all this work just to feel like I'm barely making it?" What followed that question would be "Why me?!")

But it would get better.

My first emotional, physical, spiritual (radical) breakthrough, all in one, would come via Jayne's Intensive.

These pages are full of gratitude for her life's work that now culminates with this book. My life was on the receiving end of her walk when she took my hand and helped me, through the lifting of my burdens, making space for God's love and peace-the peace I was desperately wanting. It's the gift that remained and keeps flourishing.

Chapter 12

Getting Aboard the Ship Without Skinning Your Knees on the Way Up the Stairs

I was set to go to the Intensive on April 10, 2009, and I didn't know what to expect. I was afraid. What would it be like? What if I went and I felt the same way afterwards? Then what? I would really be lost! But I wouldn't let my fear of the unknown get in the way. I wanted relief.

When I look at how my struggle to feel at peace in the midst of my depression and weave it with Jayne's teachings, her abandonment theory, and how she designed the Intensive Program, what comes to mind is Sandra Cisneros' image about birthdays. She explains how at any given age, you are also all the previous years and how as we grow old we develop layers just like an onion or like the age rings inside a tree trunk. The fiber of our childhood is part of us. Our years' experiences fit one inside the other.

That is what comes to mind about the Intensive weekend I experienced. That weekend I experienced for myself that we have to go within, to those early years inside us, to be liberated from past experiences that impact us in the present at a subconscious level.

Through Jayne's activities and layout of the Intensive, she tapped directly into the heart of those early years—the only time when, she explains, we can truly be abandoned by others. Like the layers of an onion, based on my experience, going to the heart of the onion propels us forward more quickly, to deal with the layers of our present. If we don't heal those wounds, we engage in a cycle that I know all too well: self-abandonment. And it hurts.

Like the rings in the middle of a tree, abandonment wounds are more concentrated. That's where the intensity of my reactive behavior came from. Talking about my current problems, or my perception of the problems, and frustrations was not thrusting me forward. I was going in circles. Through the Intensive weekend laid out activities, and mat work, I was able to experience the alpha beta brain waves and bypass the superficial, outer layers and go to the core - not intellectually analyzing it and dissecting it, but subconsciously and consciously experiencing it. God was setting up an experience so that I could find my way. For is it not true that by the grace of God, when we seek, we find? A door had opened, and I was ready to go through it.

My Intensive was a life-changing, mood altering, anxiety-lifting event. I have always referred to it as my "I'm back" moment. Throughout the process, I was able to share my life story, to reflect on the hurts and wants and pains, and become aware that living with an emotionally-absent dad and a mom that had depression and was raised by a rager and also an emotionally-absent mom, had effects on me growing up. I became aware how I didn't feel the emotions I needed to feel growing up, and as the weekend unfolded, I mourned what I started to understand was not healthy. I connected with Nereida, that little girl that at her essence was confident, was jovial, was charismatic, was creative, was loving. I let all those body memories go. I released so much yuck and pain and it was interesting because it manifested physically at some points. I would throw up. It was a release. A physical letting go of the past and the necessary losses of my life.

And then there was also a moment of pure joy that must have lasted at least fifteen minutes. I experienced extreme delight. I remember a cell phone going off in that moment and I was in such ecstasy. Time seemed to have stood still, and I just felt warmth all through my body. I wanted to stay in that feeling. I didn't want it to end.

As the phone rang, I just remember making the connection and saying, "Oh, how beautiful. It sounds like angels singing. "Do you hear that?" I remember asking the group. From that point on, the word that surfaced for me was the word privilege. I recognized the magnitude of this moment of pure ecstasy, of a deep joy, so, so hard to describe. Somehow, I experienced a manifestation. I perceived and received an understanding that God was real and existed for me in that moment. That He was present within our very fibers. He was not simply "out there." He was right here, that He is pure Love. He is in things, in people, in relationships, in struggle and pain, in longings, in our heart's tugs and pulls. I understood how we are to find God where He is.

In an instant I experienced total love and beauty, without seeing any image to cause it. It was just part of what I sensed and became aware of. On the other side of the anger and hurt and pain that I released that one night was a rejoicing in a warm, real love that embraced me.

I had no idea that the Intensive would become the avenue by which I would have a breakthrough to spiritual healing. Up to that point, I had not linked therapy with healing, let alone spiritual healing. I just wanted others to be fixed. For me, after knowing a life of depression, anxiety, yelling as my first reaction, impatience, letting my vitality lose its glimmer, and blaming my husband and my sons for my unsettled spirit, I would say that finding peace on the other side is truly LIFE-giving. It feels like a veil is lifted. You can breathe again. That simple, glorious sense of feeling I'm going to be OK feels like coming home after being stranded on a lonely night.

Leaving the mother ship and trying to fly on my own

This is when I lived firsthand the easy phrase to write: We are mind, body, and spirit. It's connected. That weekend I realized how we fool ourselves thinking that we can nurture one and ignore the other two. Or work on two and the other one just falls into place. It doesn't work that way. I gained the understanding that I had embraced my thoughts of resentment, anger, dissatisfaction, worry, and sadness and had made them my own. These were ways I was self-abandoning. These thoughts further dimmed my spirit, and with time they manifested in my body. Our body is our indicator. It's the one that manifests the red flag. Many times it's illnesses that give that the wakeup call we need.

In one weekend I was able to grieve the pains that surfaced from my childhood. Once I was able to sit in the pain, and I mean really sit in it, and release those feelings and that sadness, the anguish was gone. I had found my voice, experienced a spiritual reconnection resulting in fervor to practice my faith in deeper ways that I had ever imagined possible.

I would never had guessed that a weekend of therapy would thrust me into knowing, with my whole body (somehow; so hard to describe) that there is a God and that all along He had been present in the midst of my path. I had faith and believed prior to this weekend. But it was as if I was invigorated, lifted with so much love that I knew in the depths of my soul that I was loved and that I had a purpose in life and that all was well.

All was how it needed to be and this day had come to experience heaven here on Earth. It's an experience so hard to describe with words. The only word that I could use for a while in describing it was the word privilege. I felt so privileged to be able to know, to confirm, in a supernatural way that God was real. That what I was taught was true. That Life just is. That it doesn't end...that it is just transformed. That we are all connected and we are all here to help each other go Home. I had new eyes that could see the depths and richness of life.

What we may not realize is that we have all of God we want. You have all of God you want. In every circumstance there is a blessing to enjoy. We just need to have the eyes to see it and the ears to hear it. When our heart is healed, we celebrate it. When we are in pain, it's hard to find the blessing.

Chapter 13

Spiritual Recovery- And Ongoing Final Frontier

It is from this point on that I have been able to be more present in my current relationships and feel strong, have a voice, and be more compassionate and joyful. I was able to see the miracles in my life. My life moved into less dysfunction, less drama, more peace, and a daily renewing of faith.

I was able to live a more abundant life from that point. This example helps me illustrate what I mean. In May of 2010, when some cases of swine flu broke out, I got on the school bus to do bus duty. The driver had on a mask and had an air filter around her neck. She was in a panic. I started conversing with her and she exclaimed, "I don't want to die." My immediate thought was, "It's interesting that she didn't say, "I want to live." To me it seemed obvious she was coming at it from a point of lacking—not abundance. A few days later I happened to watch a program on the topic of happiness on PBS. A young man was talking about how his life changed after a pool accident and was confined to a wheel chair. At one point he said something that I jotted down so I would never forget it. He said, "It wasn't about the wheelchair anymore. I wanted to live." What a contrast to the bus driver's statement. It became so evident for me that week that within the healing process, we must remain vigilant and allow life to blossom and grace us. Our approach to life, to all its holy experiences, must stem from this vantage point—from one of abundance. Not one of lacking, which for me was represented by the phrase, "I don't want to die."

My work was not over, and it still isn't, but I was able to work on my own life lessons, not the ones that I had taken on as the Hero in my family. I was able to put down the burdensome backpack that my mom and father, unaware that they had done so, had placed on my shoulders. I was little then, but I never became conscious of the load I was carrying, and no wonder I was depressed, anxious, angry, impatient, and miserable. It never occurred to me that it wasn't my husband that caused me pain, or the demands of motherhood that caused me the pain, but that I had been abandoned in many ways growing up—we all are. I also had taken on roles that had not belonged to me.

So when the Intensive was over, did I have a track of rose petals lead the way home? You know the answer. My life was exactly the same way I had left it. I was the one that was different. I felt I had a new life. I was anew. I saw my children and could perceive the great miracle of their life, their gestures. What I remember the most is being able to look into their eyes. I hugged them tight. I must have said some awesome phrase of love to my husband and I knew that we needed each other, loved each other, and were together for a reason. I cherished the family that I had. They were my teachers. They were God sent.

Continuing with the support group was key. I was able to listen to other's strengths and struggles and actions and reactions, beliefs, thinking, moments of relapse, moments of triumph, so, so much. I began to see how we had so much in common. I could see how fear paralyzed, how the severity of the abandonment wounds takes longer to heal in some cases, and how difficult it was at times to make the changes. And there were days when we could all celebrate a new action, a new thought, a new step forward that inspired each other to live more free each week. We all need a point of reference, like Jayne says.

From the day of my intensive I had started notebooks in which I wrote but mostly they were a celebration of life. I included reflections, quotes, Bible verses...bits and pieces that spoke to my soul. This is when I would share my new found voice. I would share my week and the small and sometimes big ways that I was acting in different ways, getting different responses, how I was trusting, respecting, being affectionate, showing compassion, and being kind.

I was more easily pliable, if you will. Each day I savored the new path to learning how to lean into the pain, staying vulnerable, asking for what I needed, reaching out, making different choices that took me into new directions, taking new actions, taking better care of myself, accepting the in-between phases of health and dysfunction, and more. My life began to reflect the peace that inhabited my soul. I had a renewed zest for life. Now I knew that healing was real, that God had not caused my wounds, and that his peace could reign in my heart. My journals had become my drawer to capture the holy experiences, holy moments in time that revealed to me His presence.

This is one of the entries during this period:

Saturday, May 8, 2010

As I was driving this morning back to the house, I was listening to the rattling I guess (I'm sure there's a better word) coming from the hook close to the back seat of the car made so we can hang the clothes from the dry cleaners (which I've rarely used). One of my students did a cutout out of notebook paper for my oldest son and it is the classic image of human bodies "holding hands" and they are all linked. Rafael hung it to the hook. Today it was a beautiful breezy morning and I had the windows open. I thought about him because I can hear the paper make a noise as the wind flies through. I don't see it or hear it when the air conditioner is on. I'm aware of it and smile every time we roll down the windows. I can't but help remember Rafael as I drive with the windows down.

And today, it just came to me how it's similar to our openness to God. He is there, present, but when we have the "windows closed", we are not aware, not connected. And yet the mere fact of opening the windows, we hear him, we are connected, we feel whole no matter what the circumstance. He is not a rattling in the wind of course, but I couldn't help but make that connection. So today, through Rafael's creativity, I felt God's presence in my life in this unique way and it made me aware of this great truth. This is one of those moments in life that are about true joy.....what I've read someone say is what life is about.....these twinkles of light that give us insight, perspective: we are God's children and we have a Father very real and present. We just need to roll down the windows.

And with my sons, I was more present. I was loving and celebrated my time with them. I savored pulling them close, seeing their creativity and fostering it, laugh how for our youngest son going to the mall's play section was, "Disney World" for him, I cherished their curiosity and imaginations. We shared little phrases as to how much we loved each other (to infinity and beyond is my favorite) and nurturing and guiding were important fruits of the journey.

I started this section referring to the negative tapes that play in our mind. Those tapes do change. What still creeps up is fear. But each time you do it anyway, you realize that the outcome you couldn't have even imagined it. So you still feel it but you do it anyway. It's like a muscle you begin to exercise. You feel the fear, you ride the wave, and you allow. You trust.

For me to surrender, to let go, is the most fearful thing. For a long time surrendering for me felt like giving up. It's all going to shatter into pieces and I will have nothing. That's how I felt in the one instance in my life when I thought that taking the next step forward would change my family and its existence forever. Nothing would be the same again. In anticipation to doing what I knew was the healthy thing to do, I had the feeling of complete LOSS. My marriage was over. Life as I knew it was done. In that instance letting go felt more like giving it all up. And I had to surrender to it. I had no choice. Moving forward was the only option for me.

The reverse occurred! My husband and my relationship grew tighter and intimacy, true intimacy, began to set foot in our marriage. Connection thrived, changes were made. That was the event that taught me the most about letting go and surrendering and accepting God into my relationship with my husband. It has been my point of reference. My fear of the consequence of my choice is what I feared. And it didn't happen. How our brain lies to us, how our perceptions are so limited and confined! I understand why Jayne has always shared the phrase that fear is merely false events appearing real.

"Only by going back and challenging our core beliefs can we change our feelings and responses to the world around us today." - Jayne Payne

So today, as I have experienced a lot of change in my life this past school year starting in August of 2013, I have had to recognize the fear and simply allow. I have been more easily able to surrender to life's unfolding and new directions.

In all this new journey, God's grace give us new eyes and ears to see the truths of our lives and through it all, and on the other side, to give him glory. For any circumstance has the potential to be life-giving....for Love to win. For in Love, Love wins. It's embarking on this path that allows it to happen. The name of the game is to ALLOW. Stop getting in the way. As change has come my way, I literally have learned to stop my thoughts, my perspective, the tapes that by default begin to play when I let my guard down, and say to myself, "Stop getting in the way. Allow." And when I do, life unfolds in new and better ways.

So when I am now in situations in which I become aware of the need to surrender and let go...I have a point of reference. I tap into that dreadful night when I was crying like a baby in my backyard in complete darkness with a sob as if all was lost and there was complete despair and how in fact it was the best night of radical changes in our marriage, in our common union. I gained perspective through that unraveling of events. That feeling of surrender, that used to feel like a giving up and in my gut I felt the ache and loss, now felt more like a release. Even in my body, I have become conscious that release feels like a loosening of a grip. It physically does feel like releasing. It's hard to describe. It's a release of what I mistakenly think I have control over or have a strong hold on. Mentally and physically it's a sense of let it be. Thy will be done. An act to allow. An act to get out of the way, because (by my point of reference) what I think may occur won't come to be. It's not about giving up, it's about allowing, and receiving gifts ready to be opened.

In this last year, surrender doesn't feel like it once did. Surrendering doesn't feel like I'm giving up anymore. It feels like I'm releasing. It's a release of our resistance. It's an opening to a good that is around the corner. We just block it many times. Surrendering is making space for the new, and the letting go of the past. We need to make space for it. We need to get ourselves out of the way. We need to get things out of the way. We need to get thoughts out of the way. We need to move people out of the way. We need to release our tight hold to what we think is or will be...and let go. It's not a giving up. If that's how it feels in our gut, it's not there yet. It feels like new space...for new light....for greater freedom.

Was I afraid to write this section? To share this? Absolutely. It would have been easier for me to remain in the background and only edit this book than to share. This is also a way for you to understand the growth that can occur when you heal the abandonment wounds.

Was there a guarantee you would have this in your hands? None, whatsoever. But then you look back and you recognize that all was just like it needed to be....that all served a purpose....that nothing was in vain and courage shows its face. You feel the fear, you ride the wave, and you allow. You trust. Working on this book with Jayne was a journey I didn't know was part of the plan. My crisis lead me just to just want to stop the chaos. As I have learned to make different choices in my life and weight it out until healthier dynamics evolved based on my new actions (versus reactions out of pain and wanting to be loved and accepted) life began to be manageable. I trusted myself, I felt worthy of the new changes, and I maintained my spiritual life through practicing my faith, prayer, and meditation. It's through this that I continue to maintain that life-line. Life is an unfolding of blessings—independent of how I initially perceive them to be. I know to trust. Even when I fail to do so initially....when I decide to resist. But soon serenity prevails. I trust.

If we don't learn to trust, we stay stuck. Gifts are left unopened. Too much is at stake. We have a mission to fulfill. Only we can do it. And it's not about denying oneself for others, to light out our light so others can shine. It's about knowing the magnitude of God's light in us... the magnitude of God's transformation of us—if we allow it. It's about knowing that we are not meant to walk this path alone, having the courage to reach out, to seek the path to healing (God), and then in the (unrepeatable) way we are called to make our life a gift to others. For the most majestic moments are when we realize that there was a purpose in all the threads in our life; when we discover for ourselves that life unfolds in divine order for our spiritual growth. That in every moment there was potential for Love to win. And when Love wins, we realize that God has big plans. He wants us to know we are whole in Him so that we can be his hands and feet here on Earth....and be a gift to others.

My Spaceship Has Landed, God and I are Now Aboard

The Last Ride Home

In chapter one Jayne writes about that first car ride heading home as a new born. It's in writing these lines that I began to clearly see a correlation with the heart of Jayne's message, what I experienced, and this first car ride. I can't believe I had not made this connection between the first ride home from the hospital to what we will call home to the process that I had to go through to get to a calmer side.

I had to take a ride back into scenes of my home growing up to experience those hurts one more time. But this time it would be different. I would get out the true emotion that I had failed to experience back then. I didn't know back then how to process my emotions. I was little. Very quickly, at some point, I had learned to stuff my emotions and just concentrate on my Mom's mood. I didn't know what mood she would be in. She herself had had depression when I was little. I now see how she over reacted to situations, her yelling, her sharing her pains with me....all that, with time, affected me. And as a thirty-five year old I had been clueless.

The first ride to our home our parents do for us. The second ride home, the journey to healing, we do for ourselves through the grace of God, and going Home is where we are all called.

Then when you think you have it all figured out, all is new, you realize a different dimension all together. You have the eyes to see how irony sets in. Before that, when you are in your story (whether you are aware of it or not) you are in the phase where it's about you. Your wounds. And when you are on the other side of owning your story and healing your abandonment wounds, your story seems to dissolve...to loosen its hold, to loosen its grip. Your story loses its hold and you are released into a foreign world—your present. You are released to what is truly real. You are in your present (Aaah, that's the gift of the now!), with all its potential and wonder and moments of grace and of great significance. The story diffuses and you are left with Life. The present life. You seem to take a new breath of life and you desire from your very depths to make life about others....to be a gift to others. A life of service. A life of loving, despite where others are in life. For when we love for the sake of loving, we cannot be hurt.

Once there is healing and you are living in the present, you begin to practice (and it is something to practice to be consistent) and see people for who they are. For you have done your work and know who you are. In your relationships (which have the potential to become anew) you begin to have more compassion. You don't resent success of others. You beam with them. You can more easily sit with them in their despair. You realize that they too are on a journey and that they are also in pain—they may just not know it. Because you know that without all that personal work on you, you would have responded the same—or worse. You understand that, just like you, they are doing what they can, with what they have, where they are.

Instead of judging them and being intolerant, you recognize an aspect of yourself in them. You see reality for what it is. You don't go back to your story or hurts or lacks or frustrations. You don't. You know that you know that it's not about you. It's not. Once there is healing in one area, there is healing. You don't go back. (The interesting thing is that there are always different areas to heal. The work is never done).

I could see my husband independent of our relationship. I saw him as a man. Not as the one that needed to be kind and loving and supportive...and who knows what else I had needed and had yearned for him to be. With healing, I could see him independent of me. I had the ability to recognize a man with needs and wants and desires and hurts and fears. There was a day that I felt a stream of gratitude for his patience, for his commitment. He is the man of my life. The man whose soul signed on for eternity....to walk the path. I love him forever and ever.

I could see my sister and her strength and her struggle and her soul. Her beautiful soul that had a big purpose in life and I felt the gratitude for her and the unique pairing that God had given us to walk this path together as sisters. She gets me like no one else does. She is the greatest miracle I have witnessed.

I could see my Mom independent of me and I of her. I could better enjoy her and love her and understand her and be more compassionate. I could truly love her with all her strengths and struggles. For what we are able to do for ourselves, we are able to do for others.   I am filled with gratitude for her presence in my life. She is my *Madre Santa.*

I could see my Dad for who he was today. I realized I had to make peace with him so that I could be more present in my marriage and not carry the load that had not belonged to me. I cherish my relationship with my Dad. He is such a blessing to me and so many others.

By facing all the cracks in our story, God's light shines right through.   There is a metanoia, a conversion, a release, an openness, and an incomprehensible capacity by the grace of God to see people for who they are and a desire to become a gift to them. To love. Freed from what we want them to be for us or to give us. There is a greater capacity to offer the gift in relating and interacting and loving others.

Nothing separates us from the love of God. We separate ourselves. Once we finally touch the Lord and let him touch us, we are made whole. My prayer is that we open ourselves to the graces that flow. When we go forth and love, give of ourselves, give totally....God multiplies. The act of total giving will see miracles. This is the transformation that we are called to, to receive the grace to go and love. To love one another as God loves us.

Who am I?

Who are we?

We are souls called to make our life a gift to others for Love is life-giving action. So go out and give, because it is in giving that you receive.

About the Author

Today, Jayne continues to help people break their lifelong cycle of grief and pain, proving her theory right- that if you turn within, you will never go without. She teaches others about her innovative, breakthrough process of self-healing in classrooms and speaking engagements. Now, through this book, she is sharing her breakthrough theory and her unique approach to help more people with abandonment wounds.

Jayne Payne, licensed social worker, chemical dependency counselor, teacher, creator of The Intensive Program, and author. She was also a guest in CNN's Larry King Live show because of her Intensive Program.

The highly entertaining and informative episode called *The Power of Positive Thinking* featured Jayne Payne and a panel of other distinguished guests including James Ray, President and CEO of James Ray International, Jack Canfield, the famed originator of the *Chicken Soup for the Soul* series of books, Dr. Joe Vitale, president of Hypnotic Marketing, Inc. and the founder and president of the Hypnotic Marketing Institute, and Dr. George Pratt, chairman of psychology at Scripps Memorial Hospital in La Jolla, California and co-author of *Instant Emotional Healing*.

www.theintensiveprogram.com

Notes:

1. For a thorough explanation of how our evolution can be explained by reference to the chakras, see Caroline Myss, *Anatomy of the Spirit* (New York: Three Rivers Press, 1996).

2. Research on Albert Ellie's theories of Rational Emotive Therapy and the use of ABC technique to dispute irrational believes see: *Albert Ellis "Overcoming Destructive Beliefs, Feelings, and Behaviors: New Directions for Rational Emotive Behavior".*

3. Research on Hypnosis see: Milton H. Erickson and Ernest L. Rossi, *"Experiencing Hypnosis: Therapeutic Approaches to Altered States".*

4. Shawn Talbott and William Kraemer, *The Cortisol Connection: Why Stress Makes You Fat and Ruins Your Health – And What You Can Do About It* (Almeda, California: Hunter House Inc., Publishers, 2007).

5. Research on Sigmund Freud's theories of personalities and development of the Id, Ego, and Superego see: *Sigmund Freud "The Ego and the Id".*

Made in United States
Orlando, FL
15 January 2024

42544089R00109